DANTE HALL

FACTOR

DANTE HALL
WITH
BILL ALTHAUS

PUBLISHER
PETER L. BANNON

SENIOR MANAGING EDITOR
SUSAN M. MOYER

DEVELOPMENTAL EDITOR
KIPP WILFONG

INTERIOR DESIGN AND LAYOUT
KENNETH J. O'BRIEN

COVER DESIGN
KERRI BAKER

ART DIRECTOR
K. JEFFREY HIGGERSON

IMAGING
KERRI BAKER, CHRISTINE MOHRBACHER,
DUSTIN HUBBART AND HEIDI NORSEN

PHOTO EDITOR
SCOTT E. THOMAS

ACQUISITIONS EDITOR
BOB SNODGRASS

MARKETING MANAGER
MICHAEL HAGAN

www.SportsPublishingLLC.com

Hardcover ISBN: 1-58261-796-1
Leather ISBN: 1-58261-957-3

Printed in the United States

I dedicate this book to the two most important people in my life—my mother Carolyn, the backbone of my life, and my son, Adonis, the love of my life.

—DANTE HALL

This book is dedicated to the four most important people in my life—my wife Stacy, my sons Zach and Sean and my mom, Joyce. With a support team like that, anything is possible.

—BILL ALTHAUS

CONTENTS

ACKNOWLEDGMENTS

There are so many people who made this project happen. I want to thank Coach Dick Vermeil, his wife Carol, Chiefs president Carl Peterson, special teams coach Frank Gansz Jr., my teammates and everyone from the Chiefs family who had a part in the book. My relatives and friends have always been there for me, and they were certainly there when we needed to talk to them about the book. I want them to know how much I appreciate them. There are days I wonder why I get so much attention, because without the people in my life who have loved and supported me, I wouldn't be where I am today.

—DANTE HALL

If you think Dante Hall is something special on the football field, you should try working with him. His patience, his love of life and the people around him and his ability to make the time for all things important make me respect him as a person, not just as the best return man in the history of the NFL. To Dante, Bob Snodgrass, Kipp Wilfong, Chiefs head coach Dick Vermeil, Dante's teammates, family members and former coaches—and all the folks who made this book possible—I say thank you, from the bottom of my heart.

—BILL ALTHAUS

INTRODUCTION

Dante Hall is the kind of person who is very easy to believe in.

My wife, Carol, and I have been privileged to share many special relationships with players over the years, but we're not afraid to say that Dante is clearly one of our all-time favorites. To me, Dante Hall epitomizes all the positive attributes of what it truly means to be a member of the Kansas City Chiefs. He plays the game with a passion and he handles himself with poise, no matter the situation. Kansas City fans should be proud to have an individual like Dante representing their team and their community every Sunday.

Without question, Dante is truly special, both in terms of his personality and his ability. Hey, I'll admit it. I've always rooted for the underdog. Sometimes that's a liability for me as a coach when you really get to know a kid and you want him to succeed so badly, sometimes it clouds your judgment and you make a mistake on a player. But then there are those times when that faith is rewarded—and then some—as it was with Dante. As a coach, you're constantly looking for that diamond in the rough. You want to find that kid who just needs the right opportunity to develop into a player that maybe he didn't even believe he could become. That's what I saw in Dante when I came to Kansas City in 2001.

On the outside, I could see a player whose self-confidence was shaken. In recognizing that, we started a program of rebuilding his self-esteem, thinking if he was in the right frame of mind to accept the coaching of Charlie Joiner and Frank Gansz, he would develop the ability to become a difference-maker for the Kansas City Chiefs, not only as a return man, but also as a wide receiver.

Now, never in our wildest dreams did we envision him rewriting the record books like he did. All the coaches felt we owed it to him and to the team to give him an opportunity to succeed. We all wanted him to know that number one, if he made a mistake that he had the talent to overcome it, and number two, that we'd be there to support him. There was no magic wand, no top-secret coaching technique. We just believed he could do it.

The Chiefs drafted Dante in 2000 because he had talent, that was never in question. I appreciated his talent the first time I saw him on the practice field. I'd had the experience of working with Az-Zahir Hakim in St. Louis. I remember thinking that this guy has every bit as much, or possibly even more talent as a return man than Az. Once you recognize those physical attributes, you have more patience with a guy. You don't look at what he is, but you project forward to what you think he can eventually become.

Dick Vermeil

I saw the quickness and the courage. You could tell he had no fear. It didn't take long to recognize his tremendous vision. I don't think he even knew what he was seeing on the field sometimes, he just knew where to take the football. But if a player senses you don't believe in him, he has a hard time performing at the level that will allow him to really believe in himself. That's the role of the head coach, to get everybody— the player, the coaches and the fans—to believe in him. There were some people who doubted me for putting that much faith in him. Maybe they were right, but I did it anyway.

Players like Dante Hall are the reward for me to do what I do. Ultimately, to see a young man grow the way Dante has, that's the greatest reward you can receive in the coaching profession. Wins and losses eventually fade away, but being a part of the transformation like the one that Dante has experienced, that's truly been a life-changing event. Dante transmits energy to everyone, including me. We feed off his enthusiasm and his zest for life. If you can't be passionate about a guy like Dante and what he's accomplished, you are in the wrong profession!

When we all reflect on the 2003 season, the contribution Dante made to the Kansas City Chiefs was immeasurable. He not only tied a league record by registering four kick returns for touchdowns, he also became the first player in the history of the National Football League to do it four weeks in a row! Just for good measure, he returned another kickoff for a score in the playoffs, a first in Chiefs history. Not bad for a kid who went to Europe in 2001 wondering if he was even cut out to play in the NFL.

Probably what made us most proud of Dante last year was the way he handled his newfound fame and success. Sometimes that sort of praise and attention changes a person. In Dante's case, I think it only made him stronger. It gave him a greater appreciation for his teammates and coaches who had helped him reach this level. It provided him with an opportunity to better define who he is and what's really important to him.

Over the last three seasons, Dante Hall has more than established himself in the NFL. He more or less has taken the ball and run with it. Now it's going to be fun to see how far he can go! Are there more touchdown returns in his future, or was his four-game streak the result of good fortune and good execution? Only time will tell. But in my opinion, he will continue to be very productive. His problem will be satisfying his own high expectations.

Sometimes you just have to believe.

— DICK VERMEIL

Dante and Coach Vermeil enjoy a special moment on the sidelines.

AP/WWP

CHAPTER 1

LATE NIGHT
with
DANTE HALL

One of the benefits of being a guest on *Late Show with David Letterman* is meeting other guests, like former Baywatch babe Pam Anderson.
Hall family photo

rowing up in Houston, man, I was the smallest kid in the neighborhood. But I tell you what, I had the biggest dreams. I was going to play in the NFL, or the NBA, or do something special. Big dreams, little body.

Heck, I was so small that even my nickname was small. Everyone called me 'te. Not Dante, just 'te. And that was all right with me. When you're dreaming big, you don't care what anyone else thinks.

Now, I might have had some big dreams when I was a kid. But I could have never imagined a dream this big. I mean, I'm going to *Late Show with David Letterman*. I'm not just going, I'm going to be Dave's guest.

Have you ever smiled for 24 hours straight? It takes lot to smile all day long, but that's the best way to describe it. For one great day, my mom and friends and agents spent some time in the Big Apple. And not only did I get on *Letterman*, I also got to meet my idol, Jay-Z. Here's how it all happened . . .

Members of the Kansas City Chiefs public relations staff come by every Wednesday and Thursday and give you note, any request for that week for the media. They came in that week and asked, "Do you want to do *Letterman*?" I thought they were joking with me. I said, "Come on, quit poking fun at me. You can't be serious." But they were.

I don't even remember who told me. I think it was Pete (Moris). At first, it was just, are you interested. Then, every day it's like tell me something. Tell me some-

thing. My bye week is coming up. Don't be messing with me on my bye week because I have plans to make. And I don't want to make plans for *Letterman*, then find out this is some kind of joke. I told them, if they are just playing with me, they're taking this joke too far. They were still like, "This is for real." That's when I knew it was going to happen.

Since it was the bye week, I was at home in Houston when I got the details of the flight. My mom, my agent, Brian Overstreet, my college roommate, my best friend Wayne, and some other friends made the trip. My mom and I flew first class, compliments of Mr. Letterman, and everyone else flew coach. They didn't mind—we were going to the Big Apple!

When we got there, a limo was waiting. My mom and I took the limo and my agent and friends headed over to the Meridian Hotel in a cab. As soon as I got there, *Savoy Magazine* and Channel 5 News were there. I had to do an interview right outside the hotel, but I didn't mind. My bags were still in the trunk and I was standing outside the hotel talking about Letterman. I couldn't believe it. It was like, someone pinch me to make sure I'm not dreaming.

After the interview, we just walked up and down the street. We did some shopping. Man, you just walk up the street and you can get just about anything. But that's New York. It's not like any other city in the world. Then I had to go meet some people, like the marketing lady for the NFL Network. I also got connected to meet my favorite person in the world, rapper Jay-Z, and I got to do the Don Cheadle commercial for the NFL, and I also did some things with MTV. It doesn't get any better than this.

Before I knew it, it was time to head over to Times Square. Our stretch limo pulled up to 53rd Street and Broadway and there was the Ed Sullivan Theater. They let us out right by the door, but there were a lot of fans gathered around. One lady asked, "Who's that?" Then someone said, "Dante Hall! Dante Hall!" They were all asking for my autograph, and I was happy to sign. But I don't think that lady ever knew who I was. Some guy standing next to her said, "He plays football." And she said, "I hope he's fast." That was kind of funny.

After signing a few autographs, I walked into the theater and a producer met me at the door. Then, they took me into this little room to prep me. I never saw Letterman before the show, but man, he sent all this stuff back there to be signed. I never saw so much stuff, but he sent me some nice stuff, too, so it was cool. He sent me a couple of *Late Show* jackets, t-shirts, all kinds of stuff. And you know

what the best thing about it was? I mean, it was great sitting on stage with Dave, but Pamela Anderson was on that night and I got to meet her. And I didn't just meet her, I got to hug her and I got my picture taken with her and she was wearing a robe. A ROBE! That was better than being on the show.

When I went out, I didn't really know what he was going to ask. But I think it came off really good. But you know something? People come up to me and say, "Dante, you came off as such a nice guy!" What? I watched that interview over and over. There wasn't anything especially nice about it. I was just up there telling the truth. I was just being me. It's easy to be me. People will take a lot of credit for themselves, but that's not me. I'm not going to take credit for something that my teammates helped me accomplish. When you start taking credit for yourself, that's not very nice, and I would never do that. That's just a fact. I wasn't the reason we were 8-0. Don't put me up there on a pedestal. Don't make me seem spectacular. I'm just a man, a player, who happens to be surrounded by a lot of good guys who get the job done.

"HE'S INDESCRIBABLE. HE CAN STOP AND GO AND CHANGE DIRECTIONS AS GOOD AS ANY HUMAN BEING I'VE SEEN. I'M GLAD WE DRAFTED HIM."

—Carl Peterson, Chiefs president and CEO

Who wouldn't smile if you'd just been a guest on late night television then met your favorite rapper, Jay-Z?

Hall family photo

I kind of, sort of, knew that at the end of the show they were going to have me catch a football. And I said okay, because I know they like to do crazy stuff like that. Like, when they had Troy Aikman throw a football in a moving taxicab's window, crazy stuff. And actually, what they wanted me to do when we talked on the phone was even crazier. They wanted me to stand on the roof of one building, and have a jug machine on top of another building and shoot a football from rooftop to rooftop and have me catch it—from one to the next. What I ended up doing was easier. It was all right. It was fun. They shot up a couple of footballs at the end of the program and I wound up catching the third one right there on 53rd Street. It was right at the end of the show.

After that, people asked me if I was nervous. I don't know if you can call it nervous. I can deal with football. I look forward to games. I don't think I was nervous on the show, because it was a once-in-a-lifetime deal. I mean, I went out there to soak up everything. There I was on *Late Show with David Letterman*. How many guys can say they did that? Why would I be nervous? I went out and enjoyed it. I soaked it all up. I mean, it's not like you can do it, and then come back the next night and get real comfortable. I went out and did it and had a blast, had as much fun as any time in my life. Soak it up, have fun. I didn't need to get nervous or anything, because I was having the time of my life!

During the breaks, we talked a little bit. He asked me what it was like playing for Coach Vermeil and he complimented me on my touchdowns. He seemed to know a lot about me and the Chiefs, and you could tell he was a football fan. And that was it. He was nice to talk to, but it's not like we're good friends or anything. I just looked at it as a fun deal.

To be honest I had several designers help with my clothes. I wanted to pick out something nice, not just my everyday attire. But I didn't want to go over the top, either. They made me three or four suits, and I picked one for the show and it looked good. My mom picked out my shoes. I didn't want to overdo it, but it was the only time people might see me out of uniform, so I wanted to look nice.

After the interview was over, the real excitement of the night started. I went outside, caught the football, then we were off to the 40/40 Club, which is owned by my man, Jay-Z. The place is unbelievable—60-inch plasma TVs, Play Station II, X-Box, pool tables, two or three private rooms—it's where all the athletes who are playing in New York head after their games.

I wanted to unwind a little bit, and I found out that Jay-Z was already in there. I couldn't believe it. Man, I mean, my idol was inside! He was having a drink and this manager came over and asked me, "You want to meet Jay?" And I said, "Sure." Jay had a TV on and he was watching the game and it was the first quarter. He was cool. He got up, took me around the club and showed me everything. Then I chilled for a while and came back and watched the whole fourth quarter with him.

We stayed in New York that night, and the next day my buddies and I went to Toronto. And man, it was unbelievable. I met a reporter on the previous Monday night, when we played the Raiders, and told him I might be going to Toronto. I thought while I was in New York, I might as well make the trip to Toronto. So we did, and it couldn't have worked out any better. He helped us get seats courtside to watch the Raptors play the Washington Wizards, and I met Vince Carter. Then, at the beginning of the fourth quarter, the Raptors mascot threw a ball to me and was going to try to tackle me one on one on that big, wide NBA court. Was he crazy? In front of all those people? He didn't have a chance.

After the weekend in New York was over, I thought, "I better pinch myself to make sure this all happened." It was unbelievable. But you know what was really unbelievable? There were only a few people who knew who I was in New York. It was nothing like in Kansas City, where every-one knows me everywhere I go. But what was really crazy was that in Toronto, I was shocked. I had to ask my friends, "Are we still in Kansas City?" I'd have sworn we landed in Toronto, but everyone knew who I was. I couldn't go anywhere without people talking to me and asking me about football and the Chiefs and returning kicks for touch-downs—all sorts of stuff. That amazed me more than anything. People in Toronto must watch a lot of football.

On Sunday night, we went back to Kansas City. It was the best three days of my life. But I came back to reality the next day, and I came back real fast. Coach Vermeil didn't care about any of that stuff. We came back to practice and got to work. We had a lot of football to play. We had business to do and you better be thinking about football, and only football when you go to a Dick Vermeil practice. The fun and games were over. Enjoy it later. Get to work, baby!

"THE THING THAT HAS BEEN GREAT ABOUT DANTE IS HIS DEVELOPMENT AS A WIDE RECEIVER. IT'S WELL CHRONICLED HOW HE HAS DONE AS A RETURN MAN, BUT IF YOU LOOK BACK AT THE BUFFALO GAME, HE WAS ABLE TO COME IN AND HAVE A 100-YARD RECEIVING DAY AND STRETCH THE SEAMS."
—Trent Green, Kansas City Chiefs quarterback

CHAPTER 2

DANTE HALL
on
DANTE HALL

When Dante Hall gets his hands
on the ball, anything can happen.
Scott E. Thomas photo

People ask me if I thought about playing organized ball when I was younger. There was always something going on in the neighborhood. As a kid all I ever wanted to do was have fun. I used to go outside, get a group of friends, and we'd play whatever sport was happening at that time of year. If it was football season, all the kids in the neighborhood were playing football. If it was basketball season, we were playing basketball. That's just how the neighborhood was. We had pick-up football games, pick-up basketball games—stuff like that was always going on.

Football was football to me, whether we played it in the fields or the streets or on a vacant lot. Just put some of the boys from the neighborhood out there with a ball and we were as happy as could be. We didn't have little league and all that.

I didn't play organized ball until the seventh grade. I didn't need to—we were out playing and having fun, and that's what it was all about. I believe every now and then you can have a guy who really works his way into the NFL. He might be a guy who was overlooked, or no one really knew that much about him. But I think that for the majority of athletes, it's just their calling. If it's meant to be, it's meant to be—especially in my case. I never did anything special to get in the NFL. Did I run? Did I lift weights? Nah, it's all just natural.

My cousins lived in Tyler, which was in East Texas. Everyone who lived in the community went to the same church. They lived in what we called a church community, and I went up there and was playing in one of the football games and I was killing them. I mean, I was killing them, just running all over the place, doing whatever I wanted to do. Someone said, "You can't stop that boy from Houston? How can you let him run all over you all?"

I liked that.

I was good in football, but I wanted to be a basketball player. Crazy, right? I was a basketball player, but God didn't give me basketball legs. But I never questioned anything, I was so fortunate to have the build of a football player. You might not believe this, but I was always more muscular than everyone else when I was growing up. I was bigger than the football players and the basketball players, but I just quit growing. But I was stocky and I was strong, and I could run. Oh, when I was young, I loved to run. I ran everywhere. I ran to my friends' houses, I'd run, run, run, run. . .

I didn't do anything special or out of the ordinary to get where I am. I was gifted, and now, I'm making the most of those gifts. I didn't go out and catch 100 balls a day. I went to Teague Junior High and I played quarterback. That didn't last long, though, because I never passed the ball. All I ever did was scramble. The receivers were mad, so it took about a week before the coaches noticed I could run the ball pretty well and they moved me to running back. And that's where I stayed all the way through college.

I'd found my position. I was a running back. I didn't play defense. When I went to Nimitz High School, the coaches knew

Whether he's on the field as a member of the special teams or receiving a pass, Dante Hall is a player fans can't take their eyes off of.
Scott E. Thomas photo

23

about me. Back then, we had some good running backs, really good backs, so I didn't play varsity until I was a sophomore. And that made me hungry.

But you know what? I also played basketball. It was my love. I hoped to play in the NBA, but my legs just wouldn't cooperate and grow. I saw the handwriting on the wall my junior year. Football was looking better and better, and I wasn't growing and everyone else was, so I just decided to concentrate on football. It was probably the wisest decision I ever made.

Bobby Bowden was coming down and watching me in practice, and other coaches were coming and sending me letters. I wasn't getting any letters to play basketball. Letters—oh my goodness—I put all my letters on my wall. That was my wallpaper, and I had enough to cover my entire room. My poor postman, he must have hurt his back carrying all that mail.

I'd get letters at home and letters at school. I had thumbtacks all over the wall. It was pretty cool. My buddies would ask me who I had heard from every day. It seemed like it was always Michigan. They sent me a bunch of letters. I thought I was going to Michigan, until I got hurt my senior year. My third game of my senior year I broke a bone in my foot, and the recruiting pretty much stopped from the major schools. They thought I was going to be out for the year, but I came back for the second-to-last game and I broke it again. I wanted to prove that I could come back.

I can't say it was devastating. I was upset, but devastated? Something worse than that has to happen to feel devastated. I really never get too high or too low. I can't think of anything I ever felt devastated about except when my grandmother passed away. That was devastating. This was football, and worst-case scenario I would play for a school that wasn't as big as Michigan or the other schools that were recruiting me. That didn't work out, okay. I was disappointed but never devastated.

All of the schools around here, especially the junior colleges, were trying to get me. I was just hoping an A&M or some other big school would show an interest, because I knew I was going to get healthy and that I could play. I just needed a visit. It just wasn't going to be Michigan, Notre Dame or Florida State.

Looking back on high school, it was a pretty cool time. I didn't like school for school, if you know what I mean. I liked school to see my friends—the homeboys, the girlfriends—and I had about 10 of them. That was my thing. I was always involved in something—football, basketball—that kept me occupied. When I was a kid, all I wanted to do was see my friends and hang out with them after practice.

After football was over, I went on to the next sport. I ran the 100 and 4 x100 in track. Some people could really fly, so I didn't have any state records or anything like that in track. We had to run track to play basketball. I'm no big track fan. I love to watch it, but it's hard, a lot harder than football.

Dante attracts a crowd at Best Buy as he enjoys his favorite pastime, video games.
Jessica C. Thomas photo

A proud graduate of Nimitz High School.

What I really remember about high school are the Friday night football games. Oh, high school football is so big. Every teacher, every student, everyone in town came to the games. You could close the town down on a Friday night, because everyone went to the game. And it was an event. You'd be in the bus riding to the game, and all you'd be thinking about was the event, the happening, the game that night. Fuller Stadium was a great place to play. It was the highlight of the week. Man, it didn't get any better than that. I mean, you're a high school kid playing in front of 20,000 fans—it was pure magic. It was the time of my life. I felt like the luckiest kid on earth, because I was able to experience all of that first hand. I was there every Friday night.

School would get out at 2:30. We'd all go eat as a team, get ready for the game, and take that bus trip to the stadium. We'd leave for the game around 4:30, because it was just a five-mile trip down the road. And all the way there, all you're thinking about is that game. All of the Class 5A schools played there. That's why it was such a big stadium.

It was just a special time. I think I enjoy recalling those days as much as I did experiencing them first hand. You'd get all pumped up and ready, and then, when you'd hear the band coming into the stadium sounding so good, that's when you knew it was game time. It's on.

I remember running a return back all the way in high school, and even back then, it was a pretty good feeling. People run for a touchdown, or pass for a touchdown, but there's nothing like lining 11 people up on one side, and 11 people on the other side, and this one cat is going to return the ball and you take it 100 yards—nothing like it.

"FANS ARE MISSING THE EXCITEMENT THAT PLAYERS LIKE DANTE HALL BRING TO THE STADIUM EVERY WEEK. MOST FANS ONLY SEE THE HIGHLIGHTS OF WHAT HE DOES, AND THEY USUALLY ONLY SEE HIS HIGHLIGHTS IF HE SCORES A TOUCHDOWN. EVERYBODY STANDS UP BECAUSE THEY WANT TO GET A LOOK. THEY KNOW THERE'S A CHANCE SOMETHING WILL HAPPEN. EVEN THE PLAYERS, CHIEFS AND RAIDERS BOTH, PAID SPECIAL ATTENTION WHEN HALL LINED UP FOR A RETURN. THEY ALL WANT TO SEE WHAT HE COULD DO WHEN THE BALL IS KICKED TO HIM."

—Phil Simms, CBS color analyst
and former Super Bowl MVP

CHAPTER 3

BURNIS SIMON
on
DANTE HALL

Scott E. Thomas photo

Some moments are etched into your memory. They are lasting reminders of a time long, long ago when life was simple and easy to understand.

When asked about the first time he met a young freshman named Dante Hall, former Nimitz High School football coach Burnis Simon breaks into a broad, ear-to-ear grin. He then details the moment in a deep baritone voice that would make Don Cornelius green with envy. It seems much more suited to hosting *Soul Train* than barking out instructions from the sidelines.

"You know, you have to understand the story when this guy comes in," Simon said, referring to young Dante entering the equipment room on his first day of practice. "It's equipment day, and we have all the new stuff in boxes to the right of the coaches office. And we have all the older, used equipment that we're going to give the freshmen to the left of the office. Here comes this kid, a little fellow, and he looks at the new shoes and says, 'Hey, I want those shoes.'"

Simon shakes with laughter. It wasn't the first time a youngster had asked about the new equipment, and it certainly wouldn't be the last.

"We laughed and told him, 'It's going to be a while before you get those shoes.' It was because of his size. And he says, 'Oh, I'm good enough.' We say, 'Son, that's good.'"

And they leave it like that. The days of preseason camp wind down and a freshman coach seeks out Simon.

"Now, Dante is just 14 and our freshman coach says, 'Coach, you gotta come to our first game and see this kid, Dante Hall.' I remember him from that day in the equipment room. So I decide to go check him out."

Simon arrives as the game is about to start, and little did he know that what was about to happen would impact his life forever.

"As I was walking into the stadium, Dante is back as the kick returner and he catches the ball in the end zone!" Simon said. "Our coaches are screaming, 'Stay in! Stay in!' He's seven yards deep in the end zone and he takes it 107 yards for a touchdown! I'm talking about taking it to the house the first time he ever touches the ball. And that's not the kicker!"

Not to be outdone by Hall, MacArthur High School's O'Dell James, who would soon be the No. 1 recruit in the nation, knots the score at 7-all as he returns a kick for a touchdown.

"MacArthur has to kick it back to us, and I'm wondering what Dante is going to do," Simon said. "I never dreamed he could duplicate his previous return, but he goes 103. He scores again. And he rushes for over 250 yards! And the kid, the entire time, gives the ball to the ref. As a freshman, he acted as if he was just doing his job. He makes a big play, hands the ball to the ref."

When former NFL rushing leader Walter Payton was asked why he didn't celebrate in the end zone after scoring a touchdown, he simply replied, "I want to act like I've been there before."

Scott E. Thomas photos

That comment had a big impact on a youngster growing up in Houston.

"It was like Dante was saying to everyone, 'This is what I do,'" Simon said. "He was no nonsense. I wanted to pull him up to varsity immediately. But we couldn't do it, we didn't want to rush him."

Hall became the most talked about freshman in Houston, with seven returns for touchdowns and an average of over 150 yards rushing per game.

"Oh, he got new shoes—whatever he wanted!" Simon said. "We made sure that whatever Dante Hall needed, he got."

But the lightning-quick whippet of a freshman made no demands. He didn't want anything that his teammates didn't have.

"That's what was so pure about him," the coach said. "He didn't want anything that anyone else didn't get. In the off season, we put him into the varsity athletic period. At that point, he came in and his work ethic was unbelievable. Our staff was thinking this kid is good enough to

play Division I one day. The way he came in and worked like a pack mule, never saying a word, he's a normal kid, doing what he's supposed to be doing, but he's not an average player, he's a great, great player."

Hall didn't wait long to prove to everyone that he was going to be special his sophomore year. He had returns of 88 and 95 yards for touchdowns and rushed for 106 yards in a 35-21 win over Conroe High School.

He followed that performance with a four-touchdown display in a 42-10 win over Sam Houston. He opened the game with a 75-yard touchdown and carried the ball just seven times.

"You had to look at Dante running full speed to realize just how special he was," Simon said. "And he still does it on Sunday. He runs full speed and his body is moving all kind of different directions and he never breaks stride. That's why he's going to be the greatest return man of all time. He has the speed of a Billy 'White Shoes' Johnson, but no one has Dante's balance. I don't even know if

Scott E. Thomas photos

you'd even call it balance. He's moving 100 different ways while he's running full speed."

Like a floodgate that's been opened, Simon is soon awash with memories of the young man who put Nimitz High School in the spotlight back in 1994. "I distinctly remember this," he said. "He's 15 years old and rushes for 256 yards. And you have to remember there are 17,000 to 20,000 fans in the stands and they are all hollering. He comes to the sidelines as we leave the field and he says, 'Those guys are good.' I look at him and say, 'Son, you don't know how damned good you are.' And he didn't."

As good as he was on the field, Hall made an even bigger impact on his coach after the game ended. The sophomore was approached by many of his teammates. They all wanted to know how he was going to celebrate his big game.

"They were asking, 'What are you going to do? Where are you going to go?'" Simon said. "We get back to school, and I'm about to give him the big speech

about doing the right thing, because he's becoming a team leader, and I ask him what he's getting ready to do. He says, 'Coach, I'm going home to play video games. I can't wait.'"

The comment caught Simon off guard. He would have to wait for the big speech.

"He's All-District, a preseason All-State guy, and I could go on and on and on about this guy," Simon said. "I had guys calling me, newspaper guys, asking if the sophomore is for real. I say yes, because he's playing against guys who are going Division I. It wasn't a Pop Warner League. We were in one of the toughest districts in the state of Texas and he's rattling off 250- to 300-yard games."

The youngster had a return of 60 yards or more in every game. It was an average night for him to have 500 yards total offense, and he shattered every record at the high school. The Cougar closest to touching Hall's marks was Quentin Griffith, who won a national championship at Oklahoma.

"That was the year we started talking to Dante about the chance of going to any college in the country," Simon said. "He wasn't a bad student, he just needed a little nudge, and we had some teachers there who knew that Dante was really smart. We were in a pretty simple offense—Dante left, Dante right—an I-back offense. He was so genuine, he'd come to me and ask, 'Do you really think I have a chance to play in college?' I said, 'Son, you have the chance to play on Sundays.'

"You should have seen the smile on his face. He began to work even harder." Hall's work ethic made a big impression on the coach and his staff.

"We had players who would watch Dante and it would inspire them," he said. "He worked hard, but he never changed. He was always level headed. The only time I ever saw him perturbed was his junior year."

Hall's best friend, six-foot-five, 310-pound defensive lineman Chris O'Bannon challenged his teammate.

"Chris calls out, 'You ain't getting nuthin' today.' The first play we run, he blows Dante up!" Simon said, chuckling. "I look over at one of our coaches and say, 'Let's see what happens here.' Well, the defense never touched him the rest of practice. I was convinced right then that we had something special. The defense never said a word to Dante, and he never said a word to them. He'd school 'em, and go hand the ball to a coach. There were a lot of guys who had ability and charisma, but they weren't Dante. He was almost too good to be true. People look for this dark side, and there's nothing there. He's a sweet kid with a great deal of talent."

After a great junior year, in which he won just about every honor that can be bestowed on a Texas schoolboy, both Hall and Simon anticipated a breakout senior year. "You should have seen the letters he was getting," Simon said. "Florida, Florida State, Michigan, Notre Dame, all the big schools wanted him," the coach said. "They would bring the letters to my office and they would cover my desk. We all knew he was going to have a great year and go wherever he wanted. It was pretty exciting."

Scott E. Thomas photos

Then, something happened. Simon's prize back was thrown a curve.

"We were playing McCullough High School and they had Larry Izzo, a Pro Bowl return man (at New England)," Simon said. "We were at their place and Dante had eight carries for 130 yards and we were on the 30 and Dante was going in for another touchdown." But something unexpected and unexplainable happened on the run.

"No one touched him," Simon said, in a voice barely above a whisper. "He made a cut, and we found out later he broke a small bone in his foot. He limped on one foot, hobbled in 25 yards for a touchdown. We asked, 'Dante, are you okay?'"

Hall wasn't about to come out of the game. He said he was fine and played the rest of the game. Afterward, Simon knew Hall was in pain.

"Even at half speed," he said, "Dante was like most guys at 99 percent. We brought him in Sunday, because we were worried. We took him to a specialist on Monday and found out a little bone was broken. I was devastated, and so was he. I brought him in and told him I didn't know why it happened. But I said that something good would come out of it."

But Hall wasn't buying it. He was frustrated, and his mother, Carolyn Hall, knew some action had to be taken.
"Carolyn Hall called me," the coach said, "and said she wanted me to be around Dante. So he moved in with me for a couple of months. And we just worked through it."

Hall savored the time at Simon's home. He immediately became a favorite of Simon's wife, Christine, and his son, B.J.

"Dante used to babysit my kids," the coach said. "He was a member of the family. I remember one night when he was staying with us, and he told my wife that he would be home by midnight."

Midnight came and went, and Dante was nowhere to be found.

"It's 12 o'clock and I'm wondering where he is," the coach said. "It's not like Dante to make a commitment and break it. It's about 12:10 and I go outside and I see his car in the driveway. He's asleep in his car. I wake him up and ask him what he's doing. He said, 'I told Mrs. Simon I'd be in at midnight, and when it was late I didn't want to come in. I was just going to stay out here.' I said, 'Get in here!'

"That was Dante. When he stayed with us, we never really talked about football. And we never talked about him. But we would talk all night about music or movies or video games."

But at every opportunity that presented itself, Hall would make a plea to return to the Cougars.

"He'd come to practice and try to say he was ready and coaches were bringing pressure to bring him back," Simon said. "We all wanted to see him play. It was his senior year and he'd only been in three games. But I wasn't going to risk any further damage. He had a great future way beyond high school."

The Cougars had an outside shot at the playoffs that year. It was the ninth game of the season and they were playing archrival Eisenhower.

"Dante comes out on Thursday and says, 'Coach, my foot feels good. I can play.' I knew that look in his eye," Simon said. "I was going to be there two hours explaining to him why he couldn't play. So I decided to use reverse psychology on him."

Instead of talking about his future, Simon told Hall to get dressed for practice. "He ran into the locker room, a big smile on his face," the coach said. "He comes out to practice—we don't have any pads on—and I tell him to go return one. He catches it and he's flying up the field, making cuts and I'm thinking he might be back.

"I ask our trainer, 'Doc, what do you think?' I now know it was hurting him. But I told him, against everything I believed, 'You're playing Friday night.'

"The plan was to put him in after the first offensive series. The very first time

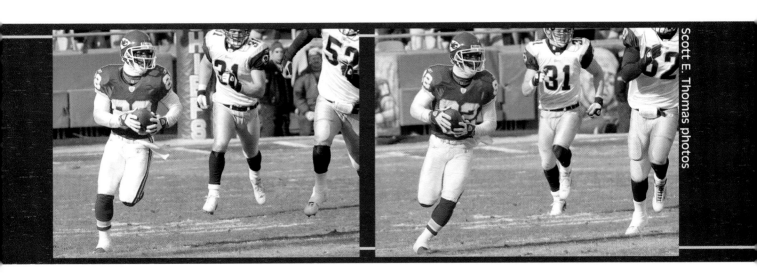

he touches the ball, he goes 60 for a touchdown. He has seven carries for 152 yards right before the half and he re-breaks it. Re-breaks it! We're up 14 while he's healthy, but we go on to lose it. The kids were deflated when he got hurt again. It was killing me."

That might have been the low moment in Simon's prep coaching career. Tears rolled down Hall's face as his coach approached him in the locker room.

"I didn't want to see his spirit get broken," he said. "I didn't want to see everything he worked his butt off for go for nothing. Three and a half games his senior year? Why?"

That question consumed Simon. But instead of wallowing in self-pity, he began to seek an answer.

"I had to start calling coaches and telling them about Dante," he said. "I had to sell him. I showed them those final seven carries. We went to work on getting him a scholarship. We kept working and making calls and sending out tapes when he asked, 'Why is this happening to me?'"

Simon didn't have the answer. But he knew someone who did.

"That's when you start talking about the motor that gets things going, the rock— everything the kid is about," the coach said. "And that's Carolyn Hall. She came in and said, 'Dante, you have worked too had. Everything happens for a reason.' And she would not let him quit. She would not let that young man veer from his mission. He stayed the course because of Carolyn Hall."

While Michigan, Notre Dame and the Florida powers lost interest, Simon called on an old friend and coaching alum.

"At the time, John Hoke, a good friend of mine, was a coach at Missouri," he said. "I called him and told him that I had a kid who might be the best player ever at Nimitz High School and one of our best all-around athletes.

"Now, he knew we had some great players. Dante was the best cover corner we had. We never played him there, because he was too valuable on offense, but it just showed what a great talent he was.

Coach Hoke looked at tape, we talked on the phone and he came down and met Dante. He said, 'We have to have this kid. He's the type of kid you want in your program.'"

Hall visited Missouri and thought he had found a new football home.

"His mother told me, 'I don't know if I want him that far away from home.' I knew where she was coming from."

So the coach plotted out a new recruiting scheme.

"I played at A&M and I called up (head coach) R.C. Slocum and I said, 'I have a great one here. You need to take a look at him.' I called Dante and told him I was picking him up and taking him to A&M."

Hall spent a few days on campus and seemed intrigued by staying in state and close to home.

"I picked him up in a couple of days," Simon said, "and he told me he liked it, he liked it a lot. That was good for me to hear. And there he went. I talked to R.C. and told him to put him at tailback and put him back to return punts and kickoffs and let him set records."

Hall was one of a quartet to rush for 500-plus yards his freshman season at Texas A&M and was setting the groundwork for an improbable NFL career.

But touchdowns and great returns aren't the only way to judge Dante Hall.

"Dante is a phenomenal player," Simon said, "but more importantly, he's a phe-nomenal person. There is a good friend of his from high school—I coached them both—and this young man decided to go down the other road. He got into trouble. I talked to Dante about six months ago and he said, 'Coach, Sherman is getting out.' I already knew what he was going to do. He picked Sherman up from prison and got him set up in a place. Dante is going to make sure he stays straight. I called Dante a few weeks later and who answered the phone? Sherman. He said Dante changed his life.

"That brought tears to my eyes. It didn't matter what mistakes he'd made, he was still Dante's friend. And Dante was going to stand by him and make sure he stayed straight."

A loving mother, a close-knit group of coaches and friends—there are many reasons Dante Hall is special. But his high school coach believes a turning point in the young man's life came at a time of great sorrow and confusion.

"Dante was 16 when his father died," Simon said. "His mother called me and said that Dante didn't want to go to his father's funeral. I called Dante and we talked, and I told him I thought it was the right thing to do."

Simon knew Hall didn't want to go.

"But I went to school and picked him up and took him to that funeral. I think it was one of the turning points in his life, because he learned to forgive. And he learned how important it was to take care of the people in his life, and to this day, he will take care of everyone in his life and all those people around him."

CHAPTER 4

CAROLYN HALL
on
DANTE HALL

Hall family photo

Carolyn Hall could pass as her son's older sister. She has even been mistaken for a girlfriend, which makes her chuckle. She is elegant and refined and the world's No. 1 fan of No. 82 for the Kansas City Chiefs.

She is watching Dante's two-year-old son, Adonis, play with a group of children in the pregame suite the Chiefs provide for players and their families. The look of love in her eyes is directed at Adonis, a beautiful youngster who seems light years beyond his age when it comes to manners and the ability to interact with other children.

In less than an hour, she will take her familiar seat at Arrowhead Stadium and cheer for her son, who has become the most captivating return man in the NFL. Sometimes she has to pinch herself to make sure she's not dreaming.

But even fame and the lure of the NFL has its drawbacks.

"It's exciting," she said. "But sometimes I wish he wasn't so famous, so we could have our privacy back. I travel to all the games with him, and we have a hard time eating in public because of all the fans wanting to come up and talk to him and get his autograph. By the time he gets through dealing with them, his food is cold and he just gets up and walks out. I'm not saying I'm not enjoying his fame, we are all enjoying it, but I wish we could have some of our privacy back."

Dante's mother is not surprised by her son's success. In fact, she anticipated it years ago.

"My mother (Katie Poole), who died nine years ago—Dante's grandmother—envisioned all of this," Carolyn said. "She predicted when he was in the seventh or eighth grade that he would go into the NFL. I always thought he was too small, that he should play basketball. But they said he was too short for basketball.

"But she saw something special in him. Imagine, saying he's going to the NFL when he was so young. I didn't think about the NFL, but I knew he was special when he used to play in the yard with cousins and friends in the neighborhood. I began to realize just how special he was when he enrolled in middle school and he excelled at all the sports—football, basketball, ran track—he even got on the swim team (laughing). And he was good at all of it. He played a little baseball, but that was boring to him. I could tell that he was special, because he was so good in everything he tried."

Even though Dante was special on the football field, he never let that affect the way he treated others.

"There were never any problems with Dante," she said. "I had a boyfriend, but I never let him discipline any of my children. No one disciplined my children but me and my mother. They didn't need a whole lot of discipline. If they did something wrong at school, all I had to do was go visit school one time and that was it, they never did anything bad again. The way he talks about his coach and teammates, the way he talks about the players who block for him, the way he treats the fans, that just shows me that what I was trying to teach him got there. He got it.

Adonis Hall and Carolyn Hall enjoy a game of catch as Dante and family members look on.
Scott E. Thomas photo

Someone told me that they were doing an interview and he opened a door for a lady. That surprised the young man who was doing the interview, because he'd seen so many athletes just walk ahead of everyone, and Dante stood back to open the door. I started training Dante and his brother when they were in the sixth grade on how to have good manners. I would stand at the door and just wait until one of them opened the door. And when we would go to restaurants, I would just stand at the table until one of them would come and pull the chair out. I was teaching them how to be gentlemen because when they met a young lady that they wanted to impress, this would help them."

Although Dante was a child who received attention because of his athletic skills, Carolyn made sure that his sister, LaShanda, and brother, Dre, were showered with love.

"I had Dante's sister when I was 16," Carolyn said. "Then I had Dante and Dre. Dre's the baby, so he doesn't do anything without asking Dante's permission. Dante is great with his brother and sister and is a great uncle. He'll pick up his nieces and nephews and take them out to eat or go shopping.

"We pick Dante's son, Adonis, up Thursday and I bring him to all the games. He is so smart at two and a half and he thinks he can get on the field and play with daddy."

It didn't matter what activity her children were involved in, Carolyn was there to support them. She never pushed them into anything they didn't enjoy and want to be a part of.

"With Dante, it was always sports. He was always ahead of the other children," she said. "I have always instilled in my children that if you are going to try for something, to try with all your heart and to give it everything you have, no matter what it is. Try to be the best. Don't be No. 2 or No. 3. He always wanted to be the best at anything."

Dante picked a great sports role model as a child.

"He was going to be another Michael Jordan," she said. "He loved basketball, but he was too short. But that didn't discourage him. It just made him try that much harder in the other sports.

Chiefs fans might look at the five-foot-eight return dynamo and wonder if he was ever the last child selected to play flag football in an elementary school gym class.

"No, oh my goodness," Carolyn said. "He was always the best athlete at whatever he did. He was the guy in the headlines once he got to high school. He was very good. People in the neighborhood had been hearing about him since he was in the seventh grade. Then, once he got in high school, everyone started hearing about him."

A smile comes to Carolyn's face as she recalls a conversation she had with her son after the first day of high school football practice.

"I remember that you had to be on varsity to get the new shoes and the new uniforms, and Dante went into high school with the attitude that he was going to get the best equipment," she said. "He went into the locker room with the attitude, 'It's me. I'm here.' And they didn't know anything about him. He said he wanted the new shoes and they had to explain to him that they were for the varsity players. And after a few games, he got those new cleats and never let the team down."

Although he was a household name in the Houston area by the time he was 14, Carolyn wanted to make sure that young Dante carried himself in a manner that would never embarrass or disappoint her or her family.

"As a young man, Dante was well mannered, well disciplined and I never had to tell him anything but once. He was very respectful. He always had a lot of girls around him, and he always handled the situation well. And if he couldn't handle it, I did." She recalled an unusual incident that took place one sweltering Houston afternoon during Dante's junior year of high school.

"I came home one day, and a mother and her daughter and another girl were in our yard talking to him," she said. "They were confronting him about who he was dating. I had to let all of them know that Dante was not married, he was far too young to get married, and that he could go out with whomever he chose. And the mother should be ashamed of herself to be involved in that mess."

While Carolyn could deal with jealous girlfriends, she was overwhelmed by the collegiate recruiting process.

"Dante has been taught not to let things go to his head," she said. "There are always disappointments out there. I taught him to stay level-headed. I tried to teach him to deal with everything and keep it on an even keel. But oh, my goodness, the phone calls and letters just got to where they were overwhelming.

"He had so many letters that he used them to wallpaper the walls of his bedroom. He got hundreds of letters, and I want to thank his high school coach, Burnis Simon, and his wife for all of their help. He really helped Dante, because my mother had died and it was a very difficult time. Dante spent a lot of time with his coach, and that was so important and so helpful."

Simon would filter out many of the recruiters who would call Nimitz High School.

"If it was someone Dante was interested in, I would sit down and take the phone call," Carolyn said. "I would set up a visit and go with him. One coach invited him to visit and I didn't go—a ticket at the last minute was like $1,000—and when Dante returned, he was saying, 'I'm going to that school.' Well, I didn't know what was going on that weekend. I decided then that that would be a school he was not going to. He thought he could go to any school he wanted, but he soon found out that I had the last say so.

Carolyn Hall believes her son is a living doll—and she's right. Well, at least he's a living teddy bear.
Scott E. Thomas photo

"He thought he could get his dad to sign, but he couldn't do that, because he didn't live with his dad. So he got a rude awakening as to who had control of his life at that time. I got to go see the University of Illinois, and I was impressed with the school, but not the weather. It was -57 degrees on the day we visited. He visited North Carolina, and he really wanted to go there, because that's where Michael Jordan had gone, and then he visited Michigan. I didn't make that trip, and when I was taking him to the airport and it hit me that my son was going far, far away. I sat at the airport and I cried and cried. I wasn't ready to turn him loose. And I think he'll probably tell you that I'm still not ready to turn him loose. I don't want him to go through the bumps and hardships of life. I'm always there to try to tell him what to do, and how to help him, and he tells me, 'Mom, I'm 25 and grown up.' But he'll never be grown up to me, he'll always be my baby."

Tears well in her eyes as she glances at Adonis, who is in the middle of a group of youngsters, having the time of his life.

"I'm sitting here thinking about it now and feel like crying," she said. "But when I was at that airport, I got to thinking that Texas A&M is a good school, and when you go to A&M you could write your ticket to any job you wanted. I told him he was going to A&M. He said he wasn't. I said, all right, go out and get a job. Now, he had a job in high school. He worked at Taco Bell, and they told him after two or three weeks that he had to work on the weekends that he played football. Well, that was an easy decision, because he didn't have to work to support himself.

The best thing about A&M was that I could get in my car and drive down and check up on him. Being a single parent, I couldn't afford to get on a plane and pay $500 or $600 every weekend to see him play. He agreed with me. In fact, after he'd been at A&M two or three weeks, we went to see him and he hugged me. Oh, how he hugged me. He was so glad to see me. He was so lonesome and so homesick. Right then, he knew we'd made the right decision. I could be there in an hour if he needed anything."

Although he prospered at A&M and became one of the most talked about backs and return men in the nation, his relationship with Coach R.C. Slocum turned sour his senior year.

"I wasn't happy with how the coach took his frustrations out on Dante," Carolyn said, a touch of disgust in her voice. "When they lost a game to Nebraska, Dante told me that some players were acting up on the plane coming home and that the coach was very upset because there were some boosters on the plane. He told me that he just put his headphones on and didn't say anything. Well, he went to a meeting with his coach and he brought up Dante's parking tickets."

Dante was well known on the A&M campus for selecting a spot close to campus and calling it his own. At one time, his fines totaled nearly $1,500.

"He called me and told me what happened with Coach Slocum. I always told my children that if you like someone and respect someone, don't say anything to them in the heat of the moment, because you can always say harsh words and you can't take them back. He just got up from the meeting and he left. The next morning, reporters were at his door asking him why he got kicked off the team."

Carolyn wanted to know the reason, too. So she made a quick trip to the campus and met with Slocum.

"I went up and talked to the coach and we had a long conversation and got everything worked out," she said. "Some reporters were willing to let Dante tell his story, but he kept quiet. It hurt him in a way, but I guess things work out for the best. We know it hurt him in the (NFL) draft. He had to go in the bottom (a fifth-round pick) and work his way back up. He was pretty mad because people said he got kicked off the team for drugs or he got kicked off the team for taking money. They were spreading all sorts of rumors that just weren't true.

"I was getting mad that he wouldn't defend himself, but then I realized he was just doing what I taught him.' I went and talked to Slocum and he did invite Dante to come back to the team, but he declined. There was just one more game and Dante didn't want to go through all that. And we knew it could have hurt him, going into the NFL. But even though he was a fifth-round pick, look how it all worked out. He got picked, so everything worked out all right—even though those first two years were tough. No one seemed to know who he was. He was never given a chance, and that hurt him."

Carolyn never knew how much it hurt her son until she received an unusual phone call.

"You want to know how badly it hurt him? He would call me and tell me not to come to his games. He felt like he was letting us down. But I told him it would be just like high school. He didn't start his first few games, but I still went. I wanted to see my son, and I didn't care what role he was playing on the team. I just hoped and prayed that someone would notice his talent."

Then, the most important development in Dante Hall's career happened, yet no one knew it at the time. Chiefs head coach Gunther Cunningham was fired and team president and CEO Carl Peterson hired his longtime friend, Dick Vermeil.

Vermeil saw something special in the undersized and underutilized return man. He wanted Dante to hone his skills in NFL Europe. Vermeil wanted him to become a wide receiver/return specialist. He envisioned great things for Dante.

"I think the biggest difference for Dante came when Coach Vermeil sent him to NFL Europe and he got to play for the Scottish Claymores," she said. "That's where he proved he could play and could help the Chiefs. And Coach Vermeil realized that, too. Thank goodness he's Dante's head coach. He's much, much more than just a coach to Dante."

It took a year for Vermeil to work his magic with Dante. In their second year together, Dante was named to the Pro

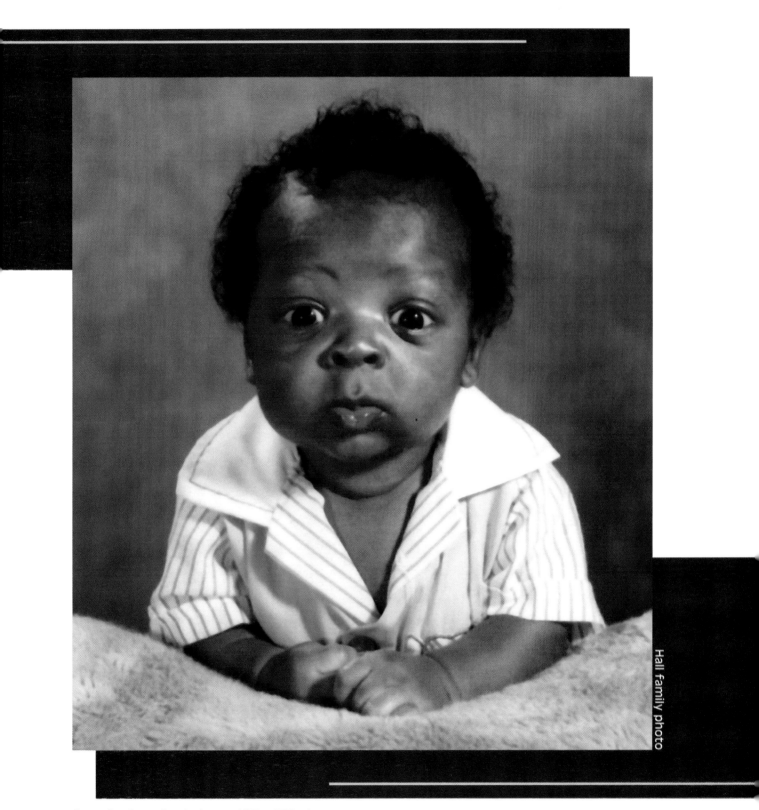

Someday I'm going to be an All-Pro NFL player.

Dante enjoys a sideline chat with teammate and fellow native Texan Derrick Blaylock.
Scott E. Thomas photo

Bowl as a return specialist. In 2003, Dante returned four kicks for scores and became the most talked about player in the NFL during the first eight games of the season. And with that success came attention—lots and lots of attention.

"Dante loves his fans, but you know he can't go anywhere in Kansas City without being recognized," Carolyn said, shaking her head. "And I've always taught him to be polite, but there have to be some limits. I think he could stand outside the stadium and sign autographs for an hour or more and still not sign for everyone who wants it. We try to limit it to the kids, because they come up and say, 'Dante, please sign.' And the adults come up and want to carry on a conversation. I'm so happy to be in Houston most of the week, so I don't have to deal with all of it.

"But now, people are coming up to me and asking me if I'm Dante's mom because they show me on TV sometimes at the games. And they want my autograph. My autograph? What are they going to do with that? Goodness gracious, I'm his mother. I haven't done anything special. Quite a few people in my building come up and ask for his autograph back home, and I just tell them that I don't bring anything to Kansas City for him to sign. That just wouldn't be fair to Dante."

Although he is one of the most visible celebrities in Kansas City, Dante can return to Houston and blend into the woodwork, hanging out with his friends and enjoying his time out of the spotlight.

"He can go home and just hang out with his friends," she said, "and if people come up to him, he can explain that he's home and just wants to be with his family and they accept that. He handles it all really well."

He also handles a knife and fork when he's home in Houston and mom is fixing his favorite meal.

"He loves steak and gravy, mashed potatoes—and they have to be real mashed potatoes, not out of a box—and green beans and red velvet cake. He hollers for steak and gravy all the time.

"The Chiefs played in Houston on his birthday this year. I had everything set up for him. He invited Derrick Blaylock and we had Dante's favorite meal and they both scored touchdowns. We were excited for Dante and Derrick.

"I just feel blessed, truly blessed, to have such a wonderful family. Our lives are very exciting."

CHAPTER 5

DANTE HALL
on
DRAFT DAY

They say good things come in small packages. Well, Dante is
a firecracker with the punch of pure dynamite.
Scott E. Thomas photo

I will never forget draft day. All my family and friends were at my house and we all just sat around and waited for that phone call. We wanted to party and celebrate, but I'd had my problems in my last year at Texas A&M, and I wasn't sure what was going to go down on draft day.

It was nerve wracking. I was sitting there and round after round went by. My hands were sweating. Nothing happened the first day. We didn't really expect it to. Then, on the second day the fifth round arrived and I got the call. We had a fax machine/phone and we gave out that number because everyone was calling on the other number and that was one call we didn't want to miss. We knew when that phone rang, we were in business. When that phone rang, my heart just stopped. My mom answered the phone, and once I saw the big smile on her face I knew we were in business.

I didn't really know who was going to draft me. I had talked to the Chiefs twice. One time I talked to the special teams coach, Mike Stock, but I couldn't tell how interested they were. Deep down inside, I think it's all about fate. Dick Vermeil was in retirement when I was drafted. All I knew about him was he came out of retirement and coached the Rams and they won the Super Bowl. Then he came out of retirement again and coached the Chiefs. But I didn't know anything about him until he got here and I got to play under him. And I thank God every day that he became the coach of the Chiefs because I don't know what might have happened if he hadn't become the head coach.

Everyone tried to create this big competitive thing between me and J.J. Moses in training camp. J.J. was a nice player. But having him in camp last year didn't change my level of play. What raised my level was that I changed my attitude. Competition on the practice field is good, but I was competing with the respect factor. The first two years here, I hadn't done anything. Nothing!

I was waiting for my opportunity. And I believe it's the coaches' responsibility to put you in a postion where you can succeed. I was not getting the opportunity early on. I wasn't used to just returning kicks. I had to get into the groove. To use a baseball term, I felt like I was a pinch hitter. I had to come off the bench to return kicks, and I needed to be in there and experience the flow of the game to really get it together.

At Texas A&M, I was a running back, I was sweating, I was in the flow of the game, and when it came time for a punt or kick return, I was ready. I felt like I was already a part of the game. But those first two years here, I was sitting for a quarter and I hadn't touched the ball, and I had to go into the game and it was tough. It's just not something I was used to. I just wasn't comfortable.

The first thing Coach Vermeil told me was, "You're my Az." That's why I respect him to this day. He told me that in his office. He told me I could be his Az-Hakim. I thought he was full of it, just like any other coach. But we started mini-camp, and I was actually in the mix. It was the first time I was a part of the offense. I wasn't starting, but I was getting reps. Before, I wasn't even getting any reps. I was on the scout team the first couple of years. I didn't feel like my career was going anywhere.

Then Coach Vermeil arrived on the scene and everything changed. Coach Vermeil and I developed this special relationship. I can't pinpoint when it happened, but my life changed. It's like asking you when you fell in love with your wife. It just kind of grew day by day. Today, if I don't have a good game, I feel like I let him down—every time—and that's tough. I play for this team and I play for my teammates and the fans—but I play for that man, and I never want to disappoint him.

The coaches tell us all the time to find something to play for. Some guys play for fame, some guys play only for the money. Some play for the fans—but for me, he's No. 1. I don't want to let him down. I don't care what anyone says or thinks—that's how I feel. It all starts with him, then it goes to family, teammates, fans, money, whatever. I know Carl (Peterson) drafted me, but he didn't stick his neck out for me like Coach did, so I say it all starts with him. As long as he's happy, I'm happy. Maybe I shouldn't say that, but that's how I feel.

I haven't told this to many people, but when I came back from playing for the Scottish Claymores, Coach Vermeil and his wife, Carol, did something that I'll never forget. I don't even know if they remember it, but I'll never forget it. It was one of those moments when you realize you have more than a coach and player relationship.

I had had an argument with my child's mother. And you know how you get so mad you cry? It takes a lot for me to cry. I cry when I'm mad, not when I'm sad. I was so mad I was furious. I couldn't see him, because I didn't want to see her. It was bad, I was crying, I was hurting, it was a tough time.

We had just come down to Kansas City from training camp and we were going to that luncheon where the fans get the chance to meet the team. Lamar Hunt was speaking and some of the players got up and talked, and all I could think about was how I couldn't see my son. When the thing was over, Coach and his wife came up to me as were walking to the bus. They knew something was wrong, but I really didn't want to talk about it.

Then, I got a call about 9 o'clock that night, and I was shocked. It was from Mrs. Vermeil. She wanted to know how I was doing. She called and said she had been thinking about me and wanted to know what was really wrong. So we started talking, and it was like a counseling session. She was so cool, and said how their son had kind of gone through the same thing and it just made me feel so good. How many coaches' wives would call a player, especially a player like me who hadn't really done anything for the team or her husband, to see how he was doing?

Coach talked to me, too. He really cares about his players. He is a great motivator and an emotional coach. People might get on him because he cries, but he cries because he really cares. Other people don't cry because they don't care. After I scored my first touchdown on a return, he was there, waiting for me on the sidelines. He gave me a big hug and it was like a natural high. That's one of the best experiences of my life.

Scott E. Thomas photos

Dante and his buddies watch a little NFL action in his Kansas City apartment.

When I look back at the last two years and think about how he stuck his neck out for me, it just makes me feel good to know that I have been able to reward him and the team. He's like a parent. He has great parenting skills. You put faith in a person, encourage him and see him graduate with that 4.0—and that's what I want to do for Coach.

Do You Believe in Dreams? I Do!

So many wonderful things happened to me last season, but the game in Houston was one I'll never forget. And it had nothing to do with J.J. Moses, even though he had signed with Houston after he was released by the Chiefs. I had a dream about the Houston game. I first looked at the schedule in the off season and I saw we played in Houston on my birthday! I had to take one back to the house on my birthday. I just had to make that happen. Then I had a dream about it. I didn't tell anyone, because I believe if you tell someone your dream, it won't come true. Then we went down there and it happened. How about that—that dream did come true!

And the way it happened made it even more unbelievable. They were kicking it high—five straight times—for two and a half quarters it was working for them. I wasn't going to get a chance. I'd go back on the sidelines and think that maybe my little dream wasn't about anything. Then all of a sudden, they hit one and that dream became a reality.

That whole weekend was like a dream. We got to the hotel and my best friend picked me up and drove me to the house where my mom was cooking. We ate a real good meal, then sat around and watched college football all day. It was the perfect way to spend a day before a big game. There's nothing I enjoy more than just relaxing with my family and friends.

My friends are special to me. I keep my circle small. My circle has been the same since junior high. I love to go home and be with my friends. When I get away from football, I want to get away from it. You know what I mean? I love the game, but there are so many other things in my life. They know I don't want to sit around and talk about football. I'm a movie guy.

It doesn't get any better than *Scarface* or *Gladiator*. Al Pacino's my man. And Russell Crowe and Denzel Washington—they're the best. If I'm not watching movies, I love to watch headline news or MTV. I want to know what's going on. And I have to have my music. So with me, it's not all about football.

As I sat around my home that weekend, it made me think back to my childhood. I was born in Lufkin, Texas, and stayed with my grandmother until third or fourth grade. My mom moved to Houston, so my brother and sister and I lived with my grandmother. My mom got a good job, and we moved in with her when her life became more stable. In Houston, all I was about was sports. I went to school, came home and played sports. Sports, sports, sports.

I was never the last one picked in gym class for any sport activity, because I was always the same size or more muscular than the other kids. I just quit growing when I got to middle school. It was pretty cool, because everyone wanted me on their team. That's when sports was fun. You're out with your friends and you play until your mom calls you home for dinner or it gets dark. Those were the only two reasons to quit playing.

Sitting here at home, it's easy to look back on my junior year in high school. It was unreal. Michigan, Florida, Notre Dame. I had a real good junior year but, I got hurt three games into my senior year. I injured my ankle and broke my foot. I wasn't devastated by it. I guess I was weird as a child. I took everything in stride. I never got too high or too low. I didn't feel like the NFL was in my future. I just played for fun. I knew I'd come back, get healed and worry about it later. Texas A&M was always there, but they came on the scene late because the Michigans and Floridas were where I wanted to go. A&M set up my visit at the right time. I told Illinois yes, I told Missouri yes. I had told two or three people yes. My high school coach played at A&M. So my last visit was to A&M, and he was talking up A&M all the way down there so I was ready to say yes and mean it. Then, I realized it's just an hour and 10 minutes from Houston, then they took me on a weekend with a real nice party and they spoil you to death. It's a running

Dante challenges a fan in a video game tournament at Best Buy.

back school, starting the Big 12 alliance, and for the most part, I'm happy I went there.

But A&M was hard socially. I was used to being around mostly black people. It was a culture shock. If I wanted to do this, hang out there, I was never uncomfortable, it was just different. I mean, looking back on it, college is where you find yourself. You go from a kid to this is who I am. It's like this—if you take a white kid who grew up in the suburbs and send him to an all-black college—see how he reacts. That's how it was for me. I had to adjust. I had to tap into different cultures. It taught me to open up my mind and expand my horizons.

I started traveling a lot and looking at different cultures and got away from my little phone booth of a world. It turned out well. It opened things up for me, taught me about myself. I would have had more opportunities or it might have been easier at a Southern school, but in the final analysis, it was a great choice and one I'm happy I made.

To me, college was a good life experience, but not always a fun time. My freshman year, I partied, partied, partied. I partied three or four times a week. And I got tired of that. I was looking for a steady relationship. I'd had a steady girlfriend and I had a friend—the first white girl I ever dated—so it was adapt and adjust or be without. I had a girlfriend kind of off

and on, and she was really important to me. Instead of going to clubs, which I did just about every night my freshman year, we'd drive to San Antonio to the River Walk and have wine. I went to the Renaissance Festival for the first time. That's the best education you can get in college. I learned a lot of life lessons and I am grateful for that. College helps you get away from your parents and helps you grow into an adult so you learn about life.

College also provided me with my first real taste of stardom. In high school, you are big at your school, but once you make it big in college, your world changes. I was lucky, because I had three great running backs ahead of me when I was a freshman. I didn't have any pressure at all. I eased myself onto that team. But I started having some good games when I was a sophomore and everything changed. I started my last four games as a freshman, and then had to get ready to learn to deal with the media as a sophomore. I tried to take everything in stride. I never thought I was better than the next person. If I kept that attitude, I knew that everything was going to be okay.

I'm successful on the field, and I've been around other people who were successful, and I saw how it changed them and how they acted around other people, and I knew I'd never want to be like that. Some people have been in the limelight

"BEST I'VE SEEN IN MY 14 YEARS IN THE LEAGUE."
—Denver Pro Bowl tight end Shannon Sharpe

Dante was a star at Texas A&M.
Brian Bahr/Getty Images

all their lives. Like when I first got here, there was Tony (Gonzalez) and everybody else. I just sat back and watched them. Tony is cool, and that's how I want to be if I ever get to that level.

You know, because I sign a few autographs or pose for pictures, people think I'm this great guy, but I'm just a normal guy in a high-profile profession. I can be mean, although it takes a lot to push me over the edge. There shouldn't be some big celebration when a professional athlete treats people with respect. I went to

a Christmas tree lighting ceremony and I saw this guy in a wheelchair and he was freezing. I went over and gave him my X-Factor shirt. I have 10 more in my closet at home. That's just what a person should do. What I do is normal not special. Sometimes, the attention is nice. You can get some special perks, but some days I just want to go to the mall and do some shopping. I just want my own personal time. That's why you always see me with a hood. I try to keep my identity private. Some days, you just need a little time to yourself.

CHAPTER 6

CAROL VERMEIL
on
DANTE HALL

Dante and his No. 1 fan in Kansas City, Carol Vermeil.
Scott E. Thomas photo

arol Vermeil isn't just the wife of Chiefs head coach Dick Vermeil. She's much, much more.

"I call her my assistant coach," Dick said, leaning back in an easy chair in his spacious Arrowhead Stadium office that is filled with awards, mementoes and dozens of photos of family members and friends.

Make that an assistant coach with a sixth sense.

Two years ago, Dante Hall was a youngster trying to escape the scrap heap of the NFL also-rans and make a name for himself. He wasn't a marquee player who had earned back-to-back Pro Bowl berths, he was an unknown return man battling for his life and a spot on the team.

When the team left its River Falls, Wisconsin, training site and headed back to Kansas City for a public function at a downtown hotel, Carol Vermeil could sense that something was eating at the two-year pro.

"I knew something was bothering Dante, so I called him that night," she said. "We had a wonderful conversation."

The coach made a call, too.

"That's our job, to step in. And that's where Carol steps in and helps so much. That's why I always say she's an assistant coach on my staff. She can make a contribution, and she enjoys it. She appreciates the opportunity to be part of my life because I am gone all the time.

"Sometimes kids need some reinforcement and support in handling their problems. It's our job to step in and try to help them like we would our own children or family members."

A special relationship that transcends player and coach began on that night two years ago.

"I tell the kids at Operation Breakthrough that Dante is my adopted son," said Carol, referring to one of the many charitable causes she champions in the Kansas City area. "They look at me, and I just leave it at that."

She then chuckles in delight.

While Dante's birth mother, Carolyn Hall, is the most important woman in his life, he is quick to say, "Mrs. Vermeil is my Kansas city mother."

Carol and Carolyn are also very close.

"His mother is so darling," Carol said. "He wouldn't be Dante if it weren't for Carolyn. She is very, very special and he adores her. Dante is just a people person. You can't be loved the way he's loved unless you're willing to spread it around yourself."

After an especially disappointing 45-20 loss at Minnesota, Carol Vermeil was the first person most players saw when they exited the crowded confines of the MetroDome visitors locker room.

She gave each player a hug and a pat on the back. When Dante left, she had a special word of encouragement. Before he boarded the bus, he gave her a hug. "First of all, I love him," she said. "He's one of my kids. I call them all kids, even though they think they are men. I'm sure

I thought I was an adult at that age, too. He's just genuine and has a very sweet way about him. He's receptive. He's not embarrassed to show his feelings.

"He trusts me and he will open up and tell me things he's going through. He's not the kind of guy who listens and doesn't appreciate your concerns. When you talk to him about something personal, he listens and accepts your advice."

Carol Vermeil was alongside her husband when he took two teams to the Super Bowl and won the world championship in 1999 with the St. Louis Rams. Although the Chiefs didn't get past the first round of the playoffs this past season, Hall's return magic made it extra special for the head coach's favorite assistant.

"Well, I felt very maternal. I did. He's very special. Not only to me and Dick, but to other players, too. The other night at the Maxwell Club dinner (where Dick Vermeil was named the NFL Coach of the Year), everyone came up to us—especially the other players—and wanted to talk about Dante. This little man, he's just awesome. Everyone loves Dante because he's so loveable. I am so proud of him and had confidence he could do those things. I believed in him and was screaming and yelling like he was one of my own kids.

Like Dante, Carol Vermeil has been applauded for the way she handles herself with the general public.

"I think the same thing happens to my husband, and even to me, you go places and are among people whose names aren't in the news every day—you're just like a regular person. So Dante's reaction would be just like mine. We do something that is so public, we're no different from anyone else. He is a standout and everyone loves the little guy. We all love him."

She loves him, and she trusts him.

In fact, she trusted him with one of her biggest surprises.

"Dick has said for years that he wanted to have a Porsche," she said. "I'm like, oh yeah, right. He said it right at the end of the season and it put a bug in my bonnet. I researched it, and it took me less time to pick out this car than five pairs of shoes. I looked at it, and said 'Oh, yeah.' It was the 40th anniversary edition. I got it, and I hemmed and hawed and had various plans of how I was going to do this. I wasn't going to just hand him the keys. I finally decided that on the last day of practice, I was going to have some of the guys come out and help me present it to him. So I came in to watch practice and Dante was standing on the sidelines with Trent Green and Johnnie Morton.

"I went up to them and my hands were trembling with excitement. They came out in the parking area and saw the car and came back in grinning from ear to ear.

"Dante kept saying, 'Oh, you have to get it in here.' So, we called Andre Bruce (the groundskeeper) and wondered if it would be okay to bring it in on the playing surface. He said it was all right.

"So (director of football administration) Mike White told Dante that when they gather around and have their little visit at the end of practice he would signal Dante and open up the garage door and I was to drive it in. I thought that would really be great. I got in the car and was outside the garage door and I hadn't driven a stick shift since I don't know when. Oh, I was so nervous. I'm thinking that all I have to do is one wrong thing and oops! The garage door looked like a little, teeny house door. Well, the garage door goes up and I think 'Showtime!' and I drive it in. I drove over to the circle of players where they were all gathered.

"Dick had not seen who was driving the car because of the overhead lights so I drove it into the circle. I had one of those helium balloons that say I LOVE YOU on it and I got out and handed him that and the keys. He has never been that surprised in all his life. The video guys had their cameras on and someone told them to video this. The players all cheered and clapped and they were running their fingers all over it. It was like they were blessing the car the way they were running their fingers all over it. It couldn't have worked out any better.

"Dick thought some player got a car. Dante said, 'That's the way to keep a fire burning in a marriage.' Isn't that cute? That's pure Dante. He's very much a people person. He loves what he does. I think he's so, so grateful to be in the NFL and have this opportunity and be with the guys he's with. This is a time in our lives that none of us will ever forget. And that's what life's about."

At the end of the 2003 season, Vermeil announced that he would return to the Chiefs for two more seasons.

That should give Dante many more opportunities to provide the head coach and his favorite assistant some special moments.

"It is so special for Dick to see Dante succeed," Carol said. "I loved it when he ran that first touchdown back and came over and hugged Dick. Someone snapped a picture and it was just absolutely great. It was a moment none of us—Dick and I and the players and fans—will ever forget."

"HE CERTAINLY POSES A THREAT. WE JUST WANT TO REMEMBER THAT WHEN WE'RE COVERING THE FIELD, THAT THIS GUY CAN RUN ANYWHERE AND HE'LL REVERSE HIS FIELD, HE'LL TWIST, TURN, WHATEVER. WE JUST WANT TO MAKE SURE WE SPREAD THE FIELD, GANG-TACKLE HIM, HOLD HIM, MAKE SURE HE DOESN'T SLIP LOOSE."

—Vernon Fox, San Diego Chargers safety

CHAPTER 7

DICK VERMEIL
on
DANTE HALL

Another touchdown means another hug for coach Dick Vermeil.
AP/WWP

Dick Vermeil sits in his office with a grin on his face. He asks the visitor to look at a photo of him, standing on the sidelines, hugging Pro Bowl return man Dante Hall.

"That was after the first one," Vermeil said, sounding like a father, talking about his favorite son. "He just came up and gave me this big hug. Those are the moments you don't forget."

Hall provided a lifetime of special moments for the Chiefs and their personable head coach in 2003, returning a punt or kickoff for a touchdown in four regular-season games in a row, then capping that effort with a fifth in the disappointing playoff loss against Indianapolis.

Although he was busy preparing for the draft and planning a series of visits with potential free agents, Vermeil found the time to talk about Hall and what he means to the Chiefs.

"Nothing Dante Hall does surprises me," Vermeil said. "In fact, I thought he would have a successful season in 2002. I sort of expected the kickoff or punt returns to begin earlier than they did in 2002. I knew it would come—then all of a sudden, he got one—and then it started.

"And in 2003, the confidence level he developed in being able to take one back (for a touchdown) was magnified. Then, I think, everyone on other kick and return teams realized what they had to do as a group. Dante didn't do any one of them by himself. There were great blocks and key plays made within the four in a row that enabled him to do it—along with one official not making a call he should

have made (in the 93-yard punt return against Denver). Later, there were two or three more he should have scored on, but one guy just didn't finish it properly.

"It's glaring that it takes everyone to do it. But he's the guy who gets it all started. He's the guy the other 10 guys rally around. He's the guy who stimulates Frank Gansz to keep searching for ways against specific coverage teams to break the big play. Coming into this season I anticipated him being successful. I didn't anticipate four in a row, but once he got four in a row I thought he'd get two or three more—and he should have—but he just didn't. Same things didn't happen that happened on those four—someone finishing off the final guy."

While the veteran coach expected success for his Pro Bowl return man, he never dreamed of watching him score touchdowns in four consecutive games.

No one in the history of the league had returned five for scores in one season, and he watched the pressure mount on Hall.

"No, it wasn't a distraction," Vermeil said, when asked about all the attention focued on Hall. "It created some pressure. It definitely created pressure on Dante, because I could sense it on the sidelines on game day. There was the frustration when something didn't go well—nothing more than that."

Hall's streak began in a 41-20 win over Pittsburgh. The Steelers had taken a 10-first-quarter lead when he returned a kickoff 100 yards to get the Chiefs back in the game.

"I think positive momentum-type plays occur in all games," Vermeil said. "What you do with them after they occur depends on how good that football team is. We were good enough to take a big play and ride on it emotionally to create other big plays. Because we have other people who could make big plays. I have seen and coached losing teams that got the big play from a kick returner and lost that game, which you normally don't do. Normally on a punt return, you win about 75 percent of the time, on a kick return you win about 50 percent of the time. But, because the team wasn't good enough to take that extra little lift and move it into something better, the opponent was still better. To me, even in the championship game, I'm thinking this is all we needed. We'll just keep going. The trouble is, the other side didn't cooperate and we couldn't stop them.

"Psychological momentum within the individual is something that's a very powerful thing," Vermeil said. "We see great examples of it when a great golfer gets on a run and wins two or three tournaments in a row. The self-esteem enhances the confidence and your positive vibrations within your own mind make everything flow better. That's one reason I've developed my coaching philosophy where I have tried to eliminate all fears of making mistakes. I try never to blame anyone for a specific play. That creates negative momentum and they are so concerned they are going to make a mistake, they don't relax and make a big play or have fun playing. There is too much concern about doing it wrong. With a guy like Dante, he's a sparkplug guy. He has the potential to do it in an unusual way. A receiver makes a big play, but they expect it. A running back makes a good long run, it's the same thing. But when it comes from the kicking game, it's more unusal. And the odds on punt return are one every 97 and on a kickoff return one every 193 (based on NFL statistics over a 15-year span). It's more of a psychological attention-getter.

"Dante is the most secure guy fielding the ball I have ever been around," Vermeil said. "He fields a punt with better skill and confidence than he does catching a pass, because he hasn't come that far as a receiver. In fielding the punt or the kickoff, he's the best. I think he looks at the field, he checks the field, in the final second he looks for the ball. He's the best I've ever seen, and I've seen some good ones and coached some good ones. I've been on the sidelines many times when my thought is, 'Jeez, don't fumble it or drop it.' I've never thought that with Dante. Never. He's dropped a couple, but when he comes off I just tell him, 'See, you're human.'"

The return that placed Hall in the NFL spotlight came in Week No. 5. The Chiefs were playing host to AFC West rival Denver and the Broncos held a 23-17 lead in the fourth quarter.

Hall committed the ultimate sin for a return man when he fielded a punt inside the 10-yard line, turned and ran back toward the end zone. Somehow, he eluded two would-be tacklers and stunned the Broncos and the sold-out hometown crowd with a 93-yard touchdown that was voted one of the Top 5 plays for the 2003 NFL season.

"I've had the good fortune of being around Alvin Haymond, who was a great punt returner in his time—although not as fast as Dante—Travis Williams as a kickoff returner, Ron Smith who was a kickoff returner, Jimmy Bertleson was a punt returner, Wally Henry who led the NFC and played in the Pro Bowl who played for me with the Eagles—all of those kids were exceptionally good," the coach said. "I kind of think if I took all the punt returns I've seen, the one against Denver was probably the most spectacular, but it should have been called back (because of a missed block to the back). But I can accept that, because we've had some things that should have been called and weren't, so they all balance out. Excluding that hit in the back, it's the best I've seen."

Vermeil sports an ear-to-ear grin as he talks about the return.

"Oh, he was competing," he said. "That's what he was doing. He was competing—that's him. You have to be very, very careful of overcoaching that kind of player because you can coach the big play out of him. I try not to do that with our guys. And when you do that, from time to time, there is going to be a big play that backfires. But that one bad play that backfires is nowhere close in negative to what allowing him to attack and be himself is to the positive. I think we had balls punted out of bounds, we had kickoffs kicked out of bounds, I think he was a distraction to the other team because they started approaching him differently in their game preparation.

"It's like all of a sudden, you're an offensive team and you have to prepare for a defense you've never seen. It throws you off. I believe that affects special teams coaches."

While Vermeil is known as a player's coach, some players are a bit more special.

"This kid is very special to me," he admits.

"Some guys allow themselves to be more special to you. They contribute from the other side to become more special."

Yet Hall believes his relationship with his coach is no different than those of his 52 other teammates.

"He made a statement to me that I really appreciated," Vermeil said. "He said, 'Coach, for a long time I thought you were really treating me special. Now, that I've been around for a time, I know you treat all of us special.' When someone else reciprocates back, it becomes a deeper relationship."

When Vermeil arrived in Kansas City, all the talk surrounded a battle for the return position between Hall, who had not accomplished much in the previous two seasons under former head coach Gunther Cunningham, and newcomer J.J. Moses. "When I came here, I first saw ball security," Vermeil said, when asked what he was in the former Texas A&M running back. "I saw quickness, courage, no fear factor, no concern for his body. I saw a kid who had tremendous vision. He didn't even know what he saw, he just knew where to go. Every once in a while he still makes mistakes, he gets too excited about the home run and he doesn't trust the return."

Vermeil was catching some heat for sticking with Hall, but that didn't bother the coach.

"Sooner or later, it's all going to come together," Vermeil said. "Instead of being upset and saying he can't play, or let's get another guy because he's not the player I thought he was—and I'm not patting myself on the back— I just believed there was a lot into this guy and all we had to do was get through the physical side and the mental side at the same time—and maybe even the emotional side—to get him to where he believed in himself as much as I did."

And that belief has been rewarded with back-to-back Pro Bowl seasons. Vermeil believes the Hall legacy is just beginning in Kansas City.

One day, the coach believes Hall could be as big an influence on the game from a receiving position as he is in the return game.

"He has to be utilized properly," Vermeil said. "That's one of my goals as a head coach. I let my coaches coach, but I make strong suggestions. And I think there are methods of using him that would enhance his game as a wide receiver. We should not ask him to do all the things the other wide receivers do because we don't ask the other wide receivers to field punts, other than Eddie Kennison. We should do more things that enhance him to do simple things.

"I think it will be hard for him to return four touchdowns this season, but I see him making a few more big plays in the passing game. I see him averaging close to the same average in punt and kick returns.

"He's a young man who can't say no, and people pull on him and distract him and drain some of what he has to give to his profession. He needs more preparation time. He is so caring of other people and wants to please other people so badly that they can be a distraction to his personal preparation."

"WHEN YOU'RE WORKING WITH DANTE, YOU KNOW THAT YOUR BLOCK COULD BE THE KEY BLOCK THAT SPRINGS HIM. THAT'S ALWAYS IN THE BACK OF YOUR MIND: 'IF I MAKE MY BLOCK, HE MIGHT GO ALL THE WAY.'"
—Mike Maslowski, Kansas City Chiefs linebacker and special teams standout

CHAPTER 8

DEAR DIARY:
THE 2003 SEASON

Dante signs an autograph for a fan
prior to a game in Minneapolis.
Scott E. Thomas photo

Everyone wants to talk about the play.

Fans come up to me and ask, "Dante, what about the play?" They don't even have to tell me what play they're taking about. I know it's that 93-yard return against Denver. It's been crazy. I've seen it a lot. I can close my eyes and see it in my head. My mom loves to watch it. I try to watch movies and she calls and says, "It's on again, it's on again."

We were down by six in a big, big game. We had the perfect scenario for a big return. You don't want to be down by seven, because a return for a score just ties it. I've never seen a crowd rise like that, or get that loud. I've never been a rock star, but if that's how a rock star feels, I need to pick up a guitar. I've been at games and experienced that buzz in the crowd as a fan. But to experience it as a player is unbelievable.

That's how I want to make our fans feel. It's so special, you have to experience it to really know what I'm talking about. It's the best feeling you can have, especially when people are looking at us to return one every week. When it's expected, it's really special.

I was just trying to make a play. The offense was sputtering a little bit and we needed a play. I figured I would take a chance. I got a couple of good blocks. I just kept getting dumber and dumber and dumber. I kept going back and going back and wondering what I was doing. It was a boo-boo play. I see guys do it all the time and wonder what they're doing...and there I was doing it myself.

Every return man knows that you put your heels on the 10 and stay there. You don't field a kick inside the 10. It's not like I have a green light and can field any punt, especially one on the seven- or five-yard line. But if I didn't make that play, all my teammates and coaches and the entire organization would have been on my butt. I'm thinking to myself, " 'Te, what are you doing? You're getting stupider and stupider. What are you thinking? You're messing up. Oh, great job 'Te."

I knew I was in the hole, but I was able to get out of that hole and hit pay dirt. When I get a kick or punt, I focus on the guy in front of me, but I use my peripheral vision to see the whole field. I took a peek to the left and saw a couple of my teammates. And I owe a big thank you to Julian Battle who got a nice block to spring me. I'm going to have to take care of him. I know a lot of folks are saying it was a clip, but I'll hold my tongue on that one. They missed a lot of calls on Denver, too.

You know something that makes that even more unusual is that we had a block on that punt, and it's unusual to return a punt where your teammates are trying to block the punt. The good Lord was just smiling down on me that day. You need to get the ball, do what you can...there's not even a thought process.

It's going to be fun to see what happens the rest of the season. Teams are not sticking to their tendencies, so we can get some returns in the second half. We make some adjustments and know what to expect. You better be ready to expect the unexpected. I expect teams punting and kicking away from me. I don't like it, but it's part of the game. And if it's good

Dante's pregame routine involves getting mentally and physically ready for the contest.
Scott E. Thomas photo

Adonis Hall and his daddy.

Hall Family photo

for the Chiefs, then it will be good for me. If they kick it out of bounds, we get it on the 40

There are things to do to keep them from kicking it away from you, like putting pressure on the punter. If I'm a coach, I punt it to the guy. If you don't punt it, then you're telling your guys you can't stop him. That sends the wrong message to your team. If I'm on a special team and our coach won't let us make the play, or he tells us to kick it out of bounds, I don't know how much faith or confidence I would have in myself, my teammates or my coach.

Even thought I've had some success with my returns, we haven't been able to give the offense field position like we did last year. People say our offense is struggling, but look at the teams we've played—and we still haven't lost a game. The main objective—the only thing you really have to accomplish each week—is winning. And we have been able to do that.

(Linebacker) Sean Barber addresses the team before each game, and when he speaks, you can hear a pin drop. He backs up everything he says on the field. He's become a real team leader. The offense doesn't have a rah-rah guy. Sometimes Priest speaks, and when he does, it's great. He could be a great public speaker. When he speaks, you can tell it comes from deep within.

I'm really excited about playing wide receiver. Coach Vermeil promised me he would get me more involved in the offense, and he's doing it. The defenses we have played, the 3-4 defenses with Texas, Baltimore and Pittsburgh, haven't allowed me to do the things I want to do.

But the more we practice, the better we're going to get. I made the switch from running back, but Coach Vermeil has had a lot of confidence in me. I always wanted to play offense. It's hard to sit on sidelines and not get into the flow of the game. It helps me as a return man. I feel like I'm a part of the team.

We don't hit too much in practice. Coach Vermeil does a great job of taking care of the teams. We were fresh against Denver because we took the pads off this week. Coach Vermeil is by far the best I've played for. I had a coach I was close to in high school and a coach I was close to in college, but I had never had a coach who cares so much about me personally. He cares about the individual. Don't be surprised if you see some adoption papers come up some day. I feel that strongly about the guy.

After a game or a hard practice, all any of us are thinking about is getting home to be with our families or going out and getting something to eat. But I always try to find the time to stop and visit with the fans or sign some autographs. I want to touch them in some way, reach out to them, because they mean so much to me and my teammates. I try to treat each fan in the same fashion I would want to be treated if I were in their shoes. Sometimes, it's hard—if you're going to the team bus or a meeting—there just might not be the time to stop. When I was younger, I looked up to Michael Jordan, but I could never get near him. So I know what it's like to try to meet someone you really look up to. To this day I haven't met Michael Jordan.

My first name isn't Dante. It's Damien. But have you ever seen the movie *The*

Omen? Well, I don't ever want to go by that name. My nickname is 'Te. My mom calls me Dante. She knows better than to call me Damien Dante Hall. She only calls me by that name if she is unhappy about something. Then she gives me a stare. When I get that stare, man—you know she means business. I try to call my mom every day. If I don't call her one day, I hear about it. If I call her six days in a row, she gets mad if I don't call her the seventh, but that's just because she loves me. When Adonis is away from home, I'm going to make him call me twice a day. He calls and leaves me messages every day. I really look forward to those messages. There are some days they really help me get through all I've got going on.

I know this might be hard to believe, but I have never been this busy in my life. I've been blessed by the Man upstairs and my teammates. But I'm going to look forward to the time when everything kind of slows down. I've been doing so many things that I haven't even been eating right. I know that's not a good thing, but at least I'm aware of it and I'm going to do everything I can to correct it.

My first two years I was in Kansas City I had a steady diet of McDonald's, Wendy's, Pizza Hut, then Pizza Hut, Wendy's, McDonald's. But now, I'm trying to eat better—when I get the chance to eat. I keep thinking about my mom's home cooking—homemade mashed potatoes, none of that boxed stuff, steak and brown gravy and red velvet cake. I'm getting full just thinking about it.

That MVP talk makes me feel uncomfortable. It's a team game and I know that as well as anyone. There is offense, defense and special teams. I'm just a part of a group effort, and I want everyone to know that. Don't put the spotlight on me after a big win. Put it on the entire team. The defense has bailed us out. The defense is getting us through this season. My goal isn't national media attention, it never has been. My goal is to be the best I can be. It's tough to be pulled this way and that way. I'm trying to keep a team goal in mind and that's getting to the playoffs. This is a total team effort.

JUST CALL ME THE X-FACTOR

I get a lot of letters and am always asked about my nickname—the X-Factor. It started off last year with Eddie Kennison and me. We played the X-position. Then it became something personal for me. I'm going to become the X-Factor—that key ingredient to a win that might sneak up on you. Opposing teams focus so much on Priest and Tony and Trent and Eddie that I want to be the guy who helps contribute to a win with a big play. I've been so successful because of the attitude of the players on this team, especially my teammates on the special teams. They feel like they score when I score. Their attitude is special, and it makes me feel special.

Some fans want to know about my time at Arrowhead and how I spend it with the special teams and wide receivers practice sessions. I go to each group's meetings and work as hard on my wide receiver responsibilities as I do my special team assignments. When we have a wide receivers session, that's all we deal with is plays for the wide receivers. It's the same thing with special teams. You can keep the two separate. It's all well organized, so I know exactly what I need to get done.

The X-Factor resting after another victory.

I take a lot of pride in the way I handle myself on the playing field, but the fans in Baltimore were giving it to me. They were saying, "Hey, little guy, stand up. Oh! You are standing up." It was hitting home a little bit. I got pissed. I'm a gracious guy, but when I got in the end zone after that 97-yard return I had to fire that football. I have fans come up to me and tell me that Sunday was their first pro game and that I gave them a lasting memory, and it makes me feel so good, so special. But I make sure to remind them of all the guys who were blocking for me and helping me get that touchdown.

I went the four games with returns for a score, then didn't scored against Green Bay or Oakland. The media attention is really beginning to increase. We had four or five plays that were called particularly for me, but the Raiders happened to run a coverage that didn't allow Trent to get the ball to me. A couple of times they were going to me deep, but the Raiders came out in a zone and another time he had to throw a blitz adjustment and didn't have time to get me the ball. Sometimes, the defenses cooperate and sometimes they don't. I try to keep a level head because it can be here one day and be gone the next. Once Wednesday hits, I focus on the next team.

The media crush in Kansas City isn't bad. I really like the guys who cover the team and try to make as much time for them as I can. I just keep telling everyone that it's a matter of getting the right kick and the right block and the right call, and when it all comes together, it's pure magic. I just have to do it week in and week out.

I feed off the crowd at Arrowhead. When they are chanting my name and waving those signs, it inspires me. I want to take it back for them. Sometimes, maybe I try a bit too hard and catch a punt and try to return it when I should just fair catch it. I have to make sure I do what it right for the team, and not what it right for Dante Hall.

Because of my size, people wonder if I am worried about injuries. I tell them no, because this is what I have worked for my whole life. You can be injured, but you have to go out and play the game.

"KICK THE BALL TO HALL!"

What a week. We beat the Oakland Raiders on *Monday Night Football* and someone writes a song about me and the team. I love it! It's very hot! It's called "Kick the Ball to Hall," and I like how they give my blockers some credit. You know how fired up I'd be if they play that song during a game? Can you imagine? Playing that in the stadium with 78,000 fans chanting, "Kick that Ball to Hall!" That might be too much for me to handle.

Whoever wrote it knows a lot about me and the team and how we respect and care for each other. It's real in depth about opening up holes and all that goes into scoring on special teams. It's different from Houston rap, it's Florida-type music. I think it was inspired by the Raiders, who kept kicking away from me in that 17-10 win. If they kick away, the offense can take advantage of the good field position. That's good, but not too good for me.

Come on, I had family and friends watching, my mom stayed up late to watch the game. It's frustrating when you don't have the opportunity to perform. But the main goal is getting to the playoffs, and we're 7-0 and getting closer and closer.

You know, this is the first year I've really been a part of the offense and not just the special teams. And I could tell you some stories about the piling on after a play—but this is a family-oriented book, so I think I'll just leave it to the imagination. After I'd get tackled, I had guys put knees in my stomach, hands inside my facemask. I need a helmet cam so you can see what's actually going on. I am seriously thinking about using a visor, because I don't want anything to happen to my eyes. I used to use a visor in college, but once I got to the NFL I quit using it. I don't even know why I quit, but another game like this one, and I might go back to using it.

The Oakland game was kind of strange because we felt like we were in control, but they scored 10 points in the last quarter and made a game of it. Anytime a veteran team hangs around, bad things happen.

I wasn't surprised how (quarterback) Marques Tuiasosopo drove them down the field. Coach says over and over that if you're in the NFL, you're there for a reason. I'm not surprised at how well he played (leading Oakland to all 10 fourth-quarter points). If you play in the NFL, you have the talent. I don't care if you're Rich Gannon or Marques Tuiasosopo. He raised his level of play, but we were still able to come out on top.

The game at Oakland was my first *Monday Night Football* experience, and it was great. I had the usual butterflies, but I've played in some big games at Texas A&M and some big games with the Chiefs. When you only play 16 games, they are all big. But a *Monday Night Football* game brings out your A game. You know there are 11 million people watching and you might focus a little bit more. I love a game like that.

It's easy for me to stay focused. When I'm on the field, I snap a rubber band that I wear on my wrist to stay focused. I also rub the tattoo of my little boy to stay focused. Every time I look at that tattoo, I stay focused.

Because we were on *Monday Night Football*, they did a halftime report on team togetherness. We all got together over at Eddie's house. When I see *Monday Night Football* giving me respect like they did at halftime, it's great. I think of where I've come from, and it's very satisfying to see that type of stuff.

I have never been with an organization like this one, where everyone hangs out with each other. We go over to Priest's house and he feeds us all dinner, or we go to Tony's or Eddie's and it's the same thing. Around the hotel, guys are mingling and making plans to get together and it carries over to the field.

And I think that's why we're 7-0. Dick Vermeil came here, he brought that team chemistry, and everyone bought into it. It carries over onto the field. Looking back at his first year, all I remember were his practices. They were hard, they were brutal. I think he was trying to separate the men from the boys. But as the weeks went by, you saw what he was all about. He demands a lot, but he doesn't demand any more than he gives. He works as hard or harder than any one player. And that's

what makes him such a great coach. Today, the practices aren't as long or as hard. He doesn't have to get on us about tempo at practice. We all believe in what he's doing, we buy into it, and it shows on Sunday.

I don't care how I contribute as long as I make some kind of impact in games. Any way I can contribute. When I return kicks, it's more natural. The pass plays they have in for me, I really have to focus, reading the coverage, getting to the line properly—I'm not at the point where it comes naturally. Offense and special teams are so different. I'm in my comfort zone returning kicks, because I've done that all my life. As far as getting into offense, reading coverage, getting open when Trent needs me, all those little things, I'm still adjusting. I say this all the time, and I mean it—when you have Tony, Priest, T-Rich (Tony Richardson), Johnnie Morton—I'm just glad to be in the mix. You'll never hear a complaint from me.

You're in trouble if you go out there in a game and start thinking too much, instead of just going out and reacting, you're taking away from your natural skills. That's what kind of happened to me. I went from going out and doing the things that God gave me the ability to do, to thinking, "What should I do in this situation? What should I do? What's going on?"

Coach Vermeil is structured, and he wants you to play smart. But at the same time, he tells you not to play scared. I love to play for a guy who is like that. You never want to play for a guy who is all down your throat. You play scared, you can't let it loose and have fun. He gives you confidence to go out and take a chance, do something that's not really structured. You can come back to the sidelines and you don't have to worry about your coach jumping all over you.

Although he's an All-Pro tight end and I'm a 5-8 receiver, I love to watch and learn from Tony Gonzalez. He runs routes as smooth as Jerry Rice. We have so many weapons in our offense, Al (Saunders, offensive coordinator) has the problem or the responsibility to get everyone involved.

Sometimes teams will double up Tony and triple team him. There is a lot to that.

So many teams hold him and chuck him at the line, but we get a different view from the film we watch every day. It's frustrating for a guy who wants to perform. I know Tony gets frustrated when he's held at the line the way I get frustrated when teams kick away from me.

I know one thing that's not frustrating, and that's watching the way our defense is playing right now. When Shawn Barber hit Rich Gannon on a blitz, we were all on the sidelines going, "Oooh, aaah, oooh!" You don't want to see anyone get hurt, but you love to see the guys on your team put a lickin' on someone, because everyone out there is trying to knock your chinstrap off. I've had that big hit before, and it doesn't feel good. But I feel good now because those Raiders wouldn't kick it to me. I just walk off the field smiling because we got a W.

When you're on a roll, it seems like the holes are bigger. When you get a return, the guys blocking want to do it again. When you get a big run, it intensifies your blocking unit. You get a return the following week, you know you're going to get the next opponent's best effort. They're going to be focusing in on you

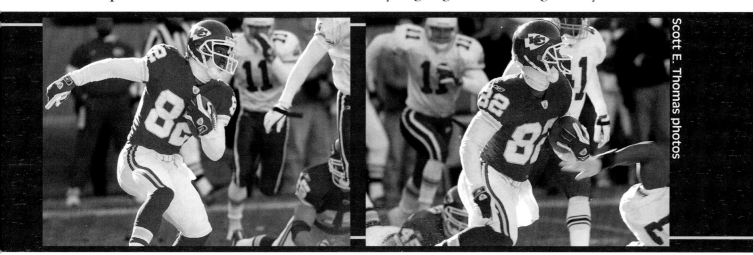

Scott E. Thomas photos

and really paying attention, but so are your guys, because they want to see you take it all the way again. We give extra effort because we love to get the ball in the end zone.

I love the respect I'm getting, but I don't think I deserve to be in that MVP talk or category because I don't get enough snaps. I'd vote for someone like a Steve McNair, a guy who can determine the outcome of the game. My hat goes off to our defense, because in so many of my returns, they have had to go out and hold a team and keep them from scoring so we can win the game.

I heard some people talking about the Chiefs being lucky. I don't know, maybe we are. But I think that hard work helps make teams lucky. Like when Marc

Boerigter hustled down the field and recovered that fumbled punt and we took it in to score (on a two-yard run by Holmes). Was that lucky? No, it was because Boerigter was hustling his butt off. All good teams have some luck, but most of them make the luck themselves. Every team needs a little luck to be 7-0, but you have to make your own luck. You have to turn your luck into good fortune.

Lucky? Who knows? Focused? You bet! We are focused, maybe the most focused team I have ever been a part of. We have a little thing called one snap and clear. Something bad happens, you have to clear it and go onto the next play. If something good goes on, like a good return, a touchdown pass or whatever, you clear it and go on to the next play. That keeps us focused and ready to go…

"TRUST ME, OUR PLAYERS KNOW WHO DANTE HALL IS. THEY WATCH ESPN. THEY ARE VERY FAMILIAR WITH WHAT HE HAS DONE AND WHAT HE HAS ACCOMPLISHED."
—Mike Sherman, Green Bay Packers coach

CHAPTER 9

DEAR DIARY: 8-0!

It's midway during the season
and we're 8-0!
Scott E. Thomas photo

LIVING LARGE AT 8-0

I don't mind telling you that I'm feeling pretty good. We're 8-0 for the first time in team history and are coming off a big (38-5) victory over Buffalo in a nationally televised game. And I scored a touchdown—but not in the way you might think.

I caught a 67-yard touchdown pass from Trent Green, and let me tell you, the fans were pumped when I took it to the house. It wasn't like scoring a kick return, that's a feeling that is just indescribable, but it felt almost as good. Trent did a great job of pumping their safety, Lawyer Malloy, off the ball. They were not handling the spread situation well at all. Trent pumped Malloy off, and all I had to do was run. He has the option to throw to anyone he chooses, and as soon as I looked back, the ball was in flight and I knew when I caught it, I was gone.

I haven't run many routes down the seam like that, and I think we caught them off guard. Because it was a 67-yarder, it was a lot like a kick return, with one difference. There wasn't a kicker to beat downfield. Once I got past the safety, I was long gone. And once I scored, I had to give the ball to (Kansas City Chiefs longtime pep band leader) Tony DiPardo. Tony gets all my touchdown balls in that end zone. He gets a bigger kick out of getting the balls than I do scoring.

I think one of the big reasons we played so well against the Bills was our week of preparation going into the game was so intense. There was a lot of talk about winning going into our bye week, but I think we wanted to prove to the world what we could do against a team the caliber of the Bills. And Denver and Minnestoa had lost, so we wanted to remain as the only undefeated team in the league.

It's a lot sweeter going into a bye week on a win than it is going into it with a loss. You don't want to sit around and think about a loss for a whole week before you get back to work. We didn't use the short week (before the Bills games) as an excuse. We were mentally and physically fresh, and the fans had us all pumped up. You could tell there was some tailgating going on as you drove into the stadium. All that smoke and that good barbecue smell. It made me hungry, but it also let me know that it was time to play some big-time football. I just love playing for this team, because we go all out for each other.

This last game was the most intense game of the season, because the energy the crowd brought got us pumped up and it got them pumped up, too. When you play in an ESPN night game, the fans are amazing. They set the tone and ignited both teams, and that made for an intense game. They were trying to be physical at the line. Baltimore was the most physical team we played this season. They were frustrated.

Once we jumped up on them at the half, I didn't see the same intensity in the second half. I think they had no confidence. The defense had seven takeaways and we scored 38 points. It was by far the most complete game by the offense and defense this season, and it's because we check our egos at the door and play to win. Just look at the season so far— defense, offense and special teams—

The real leader of this offense is quarterback Trent Green. Here he talks with the receiving crew.
Scott E. Thomas photo

we're all contributing. And that's what makes it fun.

I think one of the main reasons we are 8-0 is that everyone checks his ego at the door and we just do whatever it takes to win. Defense, offense, and special teams are all getting it done. And that's what makes it so much fun. Every time I pull into the stadium for a practice or a game, I get excited. And that excitement comes from two sources—our leader and our fans.

Coach Vermeil has really made me feel like an important part of this team. When I take it to the house, it's for him and my teammates and the fans. When I scored on that pass play, I felt like I was a part of the passing scheme. They are working me into the offense, and I really feel like an important part of the wide receiving corps. I just feel so good about everything, I wish all the fans could feel the way I'm feeling. It's something very special, something I haven't experienced before.

Football is such a team sport. When I think back to this win, I'm not going to think about my touchdown reception. I'm going to think about Trent's block on one of Priest's touchdown runs. It's just as good as seeing a linebacker sack a quarterback. Trent put his entire body on a defender when Priest scored that touchdown. You can't measure courage like that. He's awesome, totally awesome. He has as much respect from his teammates as any player in this clubhouse. I just get the chills thinking about him—to see everything develop—to see him put it on the line so Priest could score. I can ramble on and on about everything he's done. Trent is a lot like me, in a way. He

didn't start at the top. I can understand what he has been through. With me helping the team win and Trent helping the team win, I can understand it all. Dick Vermeil believed in both of us when a lot of coaches didn't.

It's all about trust. We don't meet on Saturday nights before a game. A lot of teams will get together at a hotel, before a home game, so the coaches can meet with them and keep tabs on them. But not Coach Vermeil. He brings in the type of people—not just players, but people—he can trust. We don't meet, so we can be with our families, and we're going to reward him for having the faith in us to give us that type of freedom. We have to live up to that trust. We all want that common goal—everyone has a one-track mind. And that carries over to being responsible.

I have to make a little confession. I keep hearing the rumors about Coach Vermeil leaving. No one on this team or city wants him to leave. He is a great person and a coach. He told us if we win, he will stay here. You better believe, when he talks about leaving I'm going to bring that up. I think he was talking about the playoffs because we haven't been in a while, but we're going to get there this year. We're three wins away from getting coach back. And that's everyone's goal on this team. If we keep winning, we get our coach back. I know that excites and motivates me, and it excites and motivates every other player on this team.

I'll tell you something else that excites me, although it's on a totally different level. I just got my own website. Imagine, me with a website. Pretty cool, huh? And it's a good one. XFACTOR82.com. I've had a lot of people come up and ask me where they can get a jersey, ask me questions about my son, ask some things that I really want to answer and go into some details about. But I might not have the time to do it right then, so I can tell them about my website.

My fans are so special to me. They come up and say, "Did you know you're averaging 80 yards per touchdown return?" They have to look that stuff up to know it. I look up in the stands and see the signs—KICK THE BALL TO HALL and KICK IT TO HIM—and it makes me want to please the fans. I get frustrated because I don't have the opportunity to please the fans. I have four touchdowns, and one more and the record is all mine. You get this close to a record, you can taste it.

My little clique within a clique of the team is the wide receivers. They are the first ones to congratulate me after a return. I have my boys on special teams, too. G. Stills congratulates me after a return. He loves to see me go and is right there to congratulate me in the end zone. Those are the moments you don't forget.

And I will never forget a conversation I had with one lady. It touched my heart. I let some tears loose when I talk about her. She had a son who died of leukemia. She has another son who has an enlarged heart. She can't make it to the games because she has a back problem, but she watches the games with her son on TV and she said she about jumped through the ceiling when I scored that touchdown against Buffalo.

That's why I say I play for the fans. God love them, they mean so much to me. Fans like that lady and her son are so special to me. They inspire me. I'm almost crying just talking about her. My heart is kind of racing. For me, to do something that is special in their lives is the best feeling I can get. For God to give me the ability I have, to touch someone like that, is so special. When we talk about playing for the fans of this city and how special they are to us, it's not just talk. We mean it. I have never been in a city that gets into their sports and teams like Kansas City, and that is more reason to get pumped up. It's the bomb.

And if I should ever get a big head, or not treat someone the way they ought to be treated, I have my mom to set me straight. My mom instilled in me a long time ago to always be humble. I know it's not just about me. It's about God, my teammates and coaches believing in me. A lot of intangibles go into it.

We have a goal. We have a bye week coming up, 8-0, to get away and come back fresh and ready to go for the second half. It's weird, but it's wonderful not having a loss. We don't need a loss to bring us back down to earth. We are confident, but we are going to take it a week at a time, a game at a time, a practice at a time. We're not going to go out and do anything stupid or begin thinking we're better than we are. No way, we're going to play the rest of the season like we have the first half, and hopefully, we'll get the same results. We're going to learn from our mistakes, but they are mistakes that have come in wins. Coach is so enthused, if he could put on a helmet, he would.

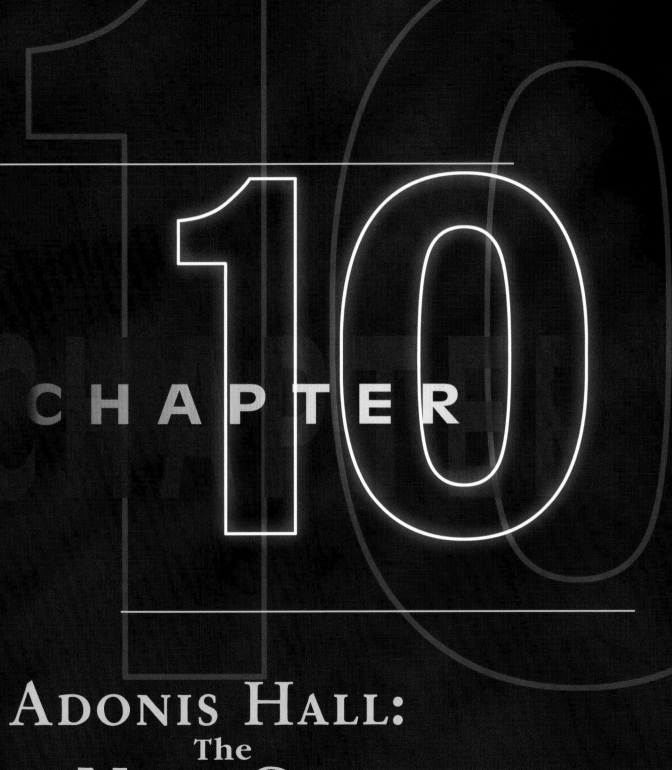

CHAPTER 10

ADONIS HALL:
The
NEXT GENERATION

A future Pro Bowler?
Scott E. Thomas photo

I really think Adonis is going to be an entertainer. I don't know what field it will be in, but he's going to be entertaining people for a long, long time. He is my first child, I'm amazed at how he sits and watches movies, just like I watch movies. You can tell he's my son. We can sit down and watch *Shrek* and *Like Mike* and he knows the names of every character in the movie.

You can put in any movie and he knows exactly what is coming up. He'll say, "Daddy, watch this," and then tell you what's going to happen, and he's only two!

The other night we were hanging out, playing dominoes and listening to Jay-Z. The people we had over were amazed that he's only two, they all thought he was at least four. He was on beat, grooving and knew the words to the music and the sound effects of the songs—at two! I was like, man, are you kidding me. This is my first, and the things he remembers and retains amaze me. It was like a little concert at two years old. He'd even pick out the songs he liked. He'd go, "Not that song, not that song, yeah, that's the song." At two, he knows what tracks he wants to listen to.

Father and son get clipped in the barber's chair.

CHAPTER 11

WAYNE EDWARDS
on
DANTE HALL

Dante Hall is equally impressive on the
playing field or at the billiards table.
Scott E. Thomas photo

Wayne Edwards recalls the first time he met Dante Hall.

Hall was a sophomore football sensation, in need of a father figure.

In stepped Edwards, who saw a side of the young man that many individuals missed.

"I think it is important to have a father figure," Edwards said. "He needed a friend, someone he could hang out with and confide in. We talked about everything—movies, football, shooting pool."

At the mention of billiards, Edwards chuckles.

"He's an excellent billiards player. For the last eight years we have had a knock-down drag-out pool series. He's at my house, or I'm at his house."

To watch Dante go from a young sopho-more with a million questions about life to an NFL star with a million return yards has been a thrill ride for Edwards.

"It's been something else," he said, "to see him go from snot-nosed high school play-er—who was pretty good in college—to what he is now. It's just special. To see him do commercials—you turn on the TV and there he is with his X-Factor Gatorade—to being considered one of the upper-echelon guys in NFL is a great feeling."

And over the course of the past 10 years, one thing has remained the same. "He hasn't changed," Edwards said. "One thing I noticed when I first met him is that he is a real grounded young man.

The only thing that has changed is the dollar figures by his name."

Edwards runs his own business, and works his schedule around the NFL season.

"It's great to travel with Dante," he said. "We went to Hawaii two years in a row (for the Pro Bowl) and we see as many games as possible. I haven't missed one home game in four years. Believe me, I have some frequent flyer miles."

Nothing Dante does on the football field shocks Edwards, who has seen just about every great return over the past two years. But there might be something about the Pro Bowl return man that does surprise Chiefs fans.

"He's unreal," Edwards said, when asked about Dante's four returns for touch-downs during the regular season, "but then you know what? Dante doesn't sur-prise me anymore. I've seen it all before— in high school or college—he's always made the big play. And he was a great running back in high school and college. He could do it all. "I'll never for-get his first return for a touchdown two years ago. He returns one all the way, then returns two the following week. On the ride back to the house, we said the floodgates are going to open now. And they did.

"And as good as he is in football, you should see him dunk a basketball. He's as proud of that as being named to the Pro Bowl. His first love is basketball. God just didn't give him basketball legs."

But God did give Dante something that everyone appreciates.

It's always a good time when Dante entertains guests.
Scott E. Thomas photo

"He's just an excellent young man," he said. "He's an avid video player. He is so intense, no matter what he's doing. He handles his business well and he takes care of the people who are important in his life. That's what I admire most about him. He handles it the same way in pros as he did in high school. A lot of guys don't remember the people they hung out with when they were non-superstars. But not Dante. He remembers who his friends are."

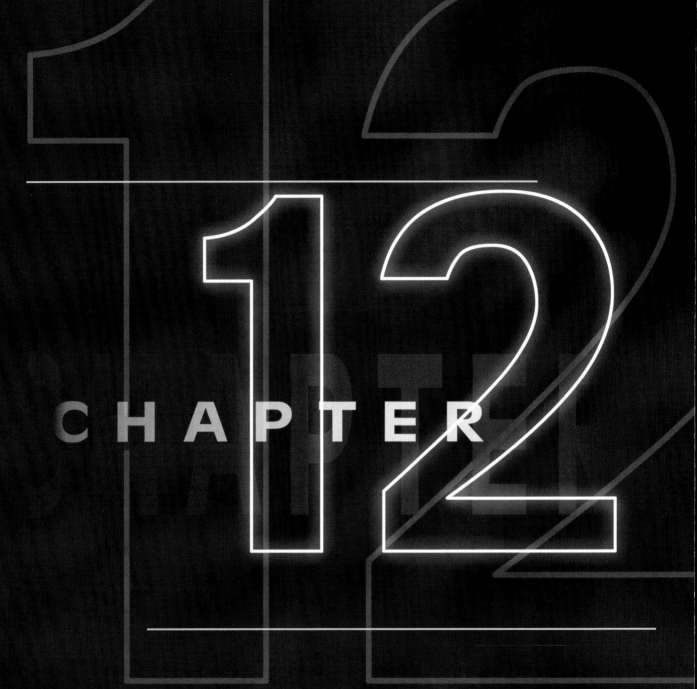

CHAPTER

12

THAD JACKSON
on
DANTE HALL

A familiar pose—Dante
and his cell phone.
Scott E. Thomas photo

Dante Hall needed a favor, so he called his favorite uncle.

"Oh, my goodness," Uncle Thad Jackson said. "I can sum up Mr. Dante Hall in one story.

"He called me one day and he said, 'Uncle, I have this girl with me. I want you to tell her the story about the buildings in Chicago.' I think to myself, 'This girl must be Cleopatra.' He was in Chicago, filming a commercial and while he was there he called and asked me where the pizza place was that we had visited before his freshman year at A&M.

"I told him where the restaurant was located and I asked him why he wanted me to tell her our Chicago story. He said he thought I would be able to tell it the way it was meant to be told, which I took as a compliment. Than I thought, 'She must be fine if I'm talking for him.'

"Way back when he was about to attend Texas A&M, Dante went with my family to Chicago. We got there and did the Lakefront and Navy Pier and the United Center and we showed him where Oprah filmed her show. Now, you have to remember that he's a young man from the South, and he had never seen anything like the Sears Tower, so we went to the top.

"We got our nose to the window, looked at all the buildings and I said, 'Dante, see that building over there? That's the Walter Payton Building. And see that one over there? That's Jim Brown. See that one? That's O.J. Simpson. I went through a couple of players who had great careers and named the buildings after them.

"Dante says, 'That's my building over there.' I told him no. So he asks, 'Where's my building?'

"We had to put our nose on the window and look all the way down the side of the building where they were digging a hole for a foundation. I mean, it was literally dirt. He looked at me and shook his head like, okay. He understood what I was saying. His building was still being constructed.

"After the first year as a freshman, he called me and asked, 'What's my building looking like now?' I said I think they poured the concrete. He said, 'They poured the concrete?' He'd set a couple of freshman records and said, 'Okay.' After his sophomore year they had the Big 12 Championship game against Nebraska and lost that game. It was a big heartbreaker for the team and Dante.

"I didn't think he was going to ask me about the building anymore, and then he runs back touchdowns in four games in a row last season for the Chiefs. He calls and asks me about the building and I say, 'I think they're working on another one now!'

"He just laughed. By the time he's done, he might have a city full of buildings."

Jackson's relationship with Dante began after the youngster's father died.

"We began to bond during the funeral," he said. "He was in seventh grade and

Dante makes his daily trip to the computer to check
his e-mail and converse with business associates.
Scott E. Thomas photo

was 12 or 13. It wasn't so much consoling him, it was more like being there for him and being his friend.

"I'd met him at a couple of family dinners and I saw how athletic he was. I knew he had the gift but never knew what to expect because of his size. We called him little big man."

The two men would talk for hours about music, and Jackson would serve as young Dante's own unique music appreciation teacher.

"I'm a musician and Dante would listen to music a rap artist would sample. I told him, 'You don't know nothing about that song.' He'd come over to my house and we'd talk about the song in question. Soon, he began to identify with old-school music.

"He'd say, 'I know you might have this song.' And I listened and sure enough I did, it was by Bootsy Collins. I started mixing tapes for him and he encouraged me to come to his games. I was living in Dallas and he was in Houston, which is about 240 miles away. My full-time job is a truck driver, so 240 miles is nothing to me.

"The first time I saw him play, I was impressed. But as good as he was in the game, I was more impressed with the way he handled himself when it was over.

"He treated everyone the same. He always had a smile, and if there was a problem, he never let anyone know about it. He played one game with a bro-

ken foot and scored two touchdowns. No one knew it was broken. He was hobbling around but was still faster than everyone."

Jackson calls Dante an overachiever, and credits his mother with helping Dante establish a strong work ethic at an early age.

"His mom did a tremendous job," he said. "I attribute his work ethic to his mom. The word 'can't' is not in his vocabulary. He had a will to succeed and that came from his mama.

"A lot of kids growing up in a single-parent household have a chip on their shoulder. But not Dante. If he had to overcome something, he did it. And he's that way today.

"Nothing has changed, He is the same guy when he comes home except he's talking on two cell phones, checks his e-mail, jumps on a computer and has a cab in the driveway for 30 minutes. That's the big change. Otherwise, it would be him asking when the waffles are going to be done."

There's that food factor again.

"Oh, Dante loves to eat. Nothing can top his mama's cooking, but we tried to get him to eat right. When we went to Chicago, we introduced to him all kinds of new food. Before he left for A&M we got him a smoker so he could smoke some chickens. I don't east fast food, and I didn't want him to, either. If all I ate were burgers, I probably wouldn't be here today. And oh, my goodness, just think what I would have missed."

Jackson had a chance to play college football, but let it slip away.

"I take so much pride in Dante, because he was able to do something that I was never able to do," he said. "I used to play football. I had a scholarship and didn't use it because of an injury. We all want to be the person who excels—whether it be as a race car driver, basketball player or the head of the class. We want to excel.

"For him to pick up one of my dreams, to get to the NFL, was phenomenal. I fell in love with his football skills at A&M. He broke all kinds of records, but he wasn't satisfied with his playing time.

"I told him, 'Dante, you have to sit there and wait your turn. When you get the ball, you run like it's your last carry. Make the most of it.' Right in the middle of the season he got the ball and I knew he was going to be special."

And Jackson can back that statement with unique documentation.

"I made a video of him from A&M," he said. "We made one with every run over seven yards from high school. We still watch that tape."

In fact, it was on the VCR draft day, that the Chiefs made Dante their fifth-round pick.

"That's what we were watching when we went to his house to see if he was going to be drafted," Jackson said. "I got there the second day. When they called his name he went in the bedroom and started praying. Now, that tells you what kind of young man Dante Hall is."

While he follows Dante's exploits in the NFL, Jackson has not yet seen his nephew in person at Arrowhead Stadium.

"I have not been to Kansas City. But I don't need to be there for him to know how special he is. Our relationship has never been scarred with an argument.

"I remember after that freshman year, there was a rumor he was going to quit school. His mother called me to talk to me. I told him that a lot of people don't have that opportunity. I thought I was going to play college ball, but I didn't. And now, I wasn't going to let him pass up this unbelievable opportunity.

"I know he's not totally satisfied with the way everything went at A&M, but you know what? He got an education and look how things turned out.

"He gets drafted by the Chiefs, and like they say, 'The rest is history.' Except for one thing—Dante is going to be writing a lot more chapters in that record book before he's finished."

CHAPTER

13

FRANK GANSZ JR.
on
DANTE HALL

Frank Gansz Jr. is one of the reasons for Dante's success. He is regarded as one of the top special team coaches in the NFL.

Scott E. Thomas photo

When Frank Gansz Jr. was a young special teams coach at the University of Houston, he heard about a schoolboy whiz from Nimitz High School.

"Everybody heard about Dante," said Gansz, who has been the Kansas City Chiefs special teams coach the past three years. "I realized he would be special in high school when I was at the University of Houston. I saw him on film and knew he was going to be a great returner. I tried real hard to recruit him, but he wound up going to A&M. He had that great reputation in high school—he was one of those guys who could score anytime he touched the ball. Oh, I knew about him. I followed him in college, but then I went to coach with the (Oakland) Raiders and I kind of lost track of him."

But the two men were reunited in Kansas City, and the end result has been spectacular. Hall was already a member of the Chiefs when new head coach Dick Vermeil brought in Gansz to coach his special team players.

"I knew the Chiefs had picked him in the draft, and when I got hired here, one of the first things I got excited about was working with Dante," said Gansz, whose father, Frank Sr., was a former head and special teams coach of the Chiefs. "I wanted to find out what he was all about."

It didn't take long for Gansz to realize that he had a special player in the former A&M standout.

"I don't know why things didn't work out for Dante his first two years here,"

Gansz said. "I think it takes a lot of things for players to reach greatness. One of them is maturity. I think you have to understand things; you have to grow up. Coach Vermeil gave him that opportunity to grow up. Maybe he needed to be nurtured. That got him to where he began to develop a trust. Maybe in the past he had some mistrust. I don't really know, although, I do know he really trusted Coach Vermeil. In any relationship you need trust, and he got that from Coach and his staff. You see how Coach treats other people—he is honest and straight with them, and you respect him for that."

Hall has rewarded that trust and confidence with back-to-back Pro Bowl seasons. "He's a very loving kid," the special teams coach said. "You can see it in the way he is around his teammates, his son, the fans—he hates to have to turn down an autograph request. The only time he does turn someone down is when he has to get from Point A to Point B and he can't be slowed down. He just has so much to give and he's a special kid."

Gansz has worked with some of the top return men in the league and believes consistency is the key to greatness.

"There are different types of return men in this league," he said. "You look at Leon Johnson with the Chargers, who is a big, strong, powerful guy who will run through tackles. You look at the guys in the past—Tamerick Vanover had a unique combination of speed and power here in Kansas City.

"The one thing that Dante has is really good balance. He's like a running back. My idea of a great return man is to be as

No one ever said being a return man in the NFL was going to be easy.
Scott E. Thomas photo

strong as a running back, along with the quickness and hand-to-eye coordination of a receiver. To be a great returner, you have to have the great vision. A kickoff return is more like a running play, where a punt return is more like a wide-open field for a receiver. That combination is rare. There are some guys who just do kickoff returns and some guys do punt returns. He has really worked at both of them, and the players really believe in him.

I could see all the good things happen that first year and knew good things were coming. He didn't really trust himself yet, he didn't have the confidence in himself that we had in him. Do I have that gear? Is it there? Once you start to score, you have it all complete. But until you score, you don't break those barriers. And that's what he did last year—he broke barriers. And he continues to break them this year."

Hall's returns have earned the respect of his teammates and peers. He was a fixture on ESPN's *Sports Center* and single-handedly changed the way opponents prepared for the Chiefs.

"It's his talent and vision," Gansz said. "He can see and feel, but he has a great deal of talent. The lift he gives us is huge. It's 10-0 against Pittsburgh and they kick off and he takes it back 100 yards. That's a huge lift to a team. I remember that one and the 93-yard punt return against Denver as the two loudest experiences I've ever heard at Arrowhead—and I've been here many times. The Denver one was probably the loudest I ever heard. I remember when I was coming off the field, a reporter told me that everyone

cheered in the press box and no one said a thing about it. You had just experienced greatness, and everybody was just in awe of the situation. Even the people who weren't really fans cheered. It was phenomenal."

As Gansz talks about his prize return man, Hall spends some time at a table in the locker room, signing a number of items for a charitable event. Gansz looks at him and grins.

"It's a bonus that Dante's such a good guy," the coach said. "It all starts with Coach Vermeil. That's the way he is with the guys. All our guys are good guys; they are easy to coach. We have our little disagreements, but we respect each other. We established guidelines back in training camp. We find that if you're honest and consistent with people, you're not going to have a lot of problems. A player wants a coach who is consistent and honest with him.

"We all take responsibility. If Dante does something wrong, he'll say, 'I made the wrong cut.' And when it goes well, he spreads the success around the locker room. It's been a great year for Dante and the rest of us."

Yet with greatness comes pressure. And Gansz is well aware that Hall's life has changed forever because of his touchdown returns.

"I've noticed a few subtle changes with Dante," he said. "I think it's more outward with the media asking him about the record all the time and I kind of wish they would leave him alone. I'm from the

Dante has developed a special relationship with his fans, both young and old.
Jessica C. Thomas photo

school of thought where you are humble and say very little. Give credit to your teammates and go forward. I don't like the media on him all the time and all we want to do it to try to help our team win."

CHAPTER 14

DEAR DIARY:
GOTTA' KEEP FOCUSED

Scott E. Thomas photo

My experiences on *Late Show with David Letterman* have been well documented, but I think it's important to talk about the return from the bye week. I think we all had some questions about how the first practice would go, and to be quite honest, it was great. I was standing on the side with Johnnie Morton and we looked at each other and said, "We look pretty sharp." And we did. Guys were hustling. We came back with the mindset that we have something to accomplish. Coach told us he wanted us to get into the flow of practice. There was no pressure today. We just got back and it felt good to be back.

All the talk is about going undefeated. I'm sure there are a lot of people thinking about 16-0, but we take it all one game at a time. I think about the next game and that's it. I'm not thinking about winning game No. 16 and going undefeated. We're back after the break, we're happy to be 8-0 and now we want to be 9-0, and that's all we can concern ourselves with. The only thing that matters is the Super Bowl.

Something interesting happened at practice today as Coach Vermeil upgraded Larry Johnson to the No. 2 running back behind Priest. I don't think it's anything against Derrick Blaylock, who really played well. I think Coach thinks we have this No. 1 draft choice talent standing on the sidelines and he wants to see what he can do. We all want to see what he can do. He needs the reps. I know that from when I wasn't getting reps early in my career. Coach Vermeil wants to give everyone a chance. Plus, you need security in case something might happen to Priest. Derrick will be fine because Coach will let him know why this decision was made. It will just make us a stronger team.

9-0!

A good work week led to another win, we're 9-0 baby! We won a wild game at Cleveland a year ago, but this time, we handled the Browns 41-20. It was pretty much business as usual as Priest scored a couple of touchdowns, Eddie had a nice game with 115 yards and a score, and the defense forced a fumble that we converted into a touchdown. I didn't get in on the scoring action, but as long as we win, that's all right. Now, we have to turn all our attention to the most underrated team in the league, at least the most underrated in the AFC—the 4-5 Cincinnati Bengals.

People say they're 4-5 and that we should go in there and beat them like we've beaten every other team, but I think it's going to be a challenge. They're tough. They have some great players, and (head coach) Marvin Lewis is going to turn that program around. I just hope he doesn't turn it around this week. But we can't worry about that, we have to prepare like we would for any other opponent. And we're confident that we can go anywhere and play anyone and come away with a victory.

HUMBLED

Well, we had a good week of preparation and all felt confident before the Bengals game, but we lost (24-19). Watching them play was almost like looking in a mirror. They did everything that we had done in our previous nine games to come away with that win.

The eyes say it all: "I'm ready to go!"
Scott E. Thomas photo

They didn't turn the ball over, they were the team with the big punt return for a touchdown, and they kept our special teams out of the end zone. I know I didn't have many opportunities for a big return. They really hustled to the ball and kept me from breaking away. They kicked it to me, but I didn't get it done. You're going to have days like that.

When (Peter) Warrick ran that punt back for the (68-yard) touchdown, I was thinking to myself that they are a pretty darned good team. But I was one of the guys who said that all week long. I was also wishing I was in Warrick's shoes because I know how good that feels. They had that never-say-die approach to the game, and you have to respect that. We all would have liked to have gone undefeated this season, but this is one loss, and our ultimate goal isn't 16-0—it's going to the Super Bowl. I know this team and I know this coach, and believe me, we're going to come back stronger than ever.

I think what we needed after a loss to the Bengals was something to fire us up. And who do we play next? The Oakland Raiders. Thank you Mr. Schedule Maker. This is just what the doctor ordered. We've had a great week of practice and everyone is really in tune to the game and to getting back on the winning path.

Things are more intense the week before a game with the Raiders, and that's just what we needed. I know that to a man, we all knew we were going to bounce back this week and we did, although the Raiders made it interesting at the end. We got off to a great 14-0 lead, and Arrowhead was rocking. We took a 21-7 lead into the half, but needed a (Morten Andersen) field goal to win 27-24 with four seconds left in the game. The win was our 11th in a row at home and that's pretty special. We feel like Arrowhead Stadium is our house, and we don't want anyone to come here and feel like they can win—especially the Raiders.

Pressing On

This is Thanksgiving Week and we're all looking forward to celebrating with a win at San Diego. We had a nice turkey feast at the stadium the day before Thanksgiving, and Thanksgiving Day I just ate at home, watched some of the games and slept. It was wonderful. No one around, just me, and I didn't do a thing. There are days you need like that, and I took full advantage of it. The day after Thanksgiving, it was business as usual and we had another good practice.

We've had a week's worth of good practices, and they led to another AFC victory—28-24 over the San Diego Chargers. I hope we're not setting a trend, as we got off to a 21-7 lead at halftime and once again had to hold on at the end to come away with the victory. Priest had another monster game with 162 yards on the ground and two scores. Tony Gonzalez had two touchdowns. How would you like to be a defensive coordinator and try to come up with a scheme to stop this offense?

Trent is having a Pro-Bowl year and Tony and Priest are the best in the business. The Chargers came back and scored 17 points in the second half, but when we really needed a stop, we got it. Greg Wesley made a big interception late in the game, and the Chargers scored on the final play, to make the score look a little bit closer than it actually was. We're heading back to Kansas City with an 11-1 record and feeling good about this season.

We did what we had to do, they came on strong in the second half, but Priest is Priest. I didn't play well in the return unit. Special teams didn't play well, we take a lot of pride in what we do—and we didn't do much to help the offense start off in good field position. A win is great, I just wish we could have contributed more.

Coach Vermeil talked about how they were pumped up and really ready to play us. They were flying around out there, and I tip my hat to them. They made plays, but we made more plays. Leon Johnson had some nice returns. He was running over people, but they really didn't capitalize on the good field position. They got a couple of field goals. Trent gets touchdowns for us when we give him good field position.

After the game I heard that the loss was the first time San Diego coach Marty Schottenheimer had coached a team to a 10-loss season (2-10). Marty coached the Chiefs for a long time, but I don't think any of the guys who were here when Marty coached here cared about that. We're all looking at the bigger picture.

We got our 11th win, and our special teams coach told us that no team in the history of the league had ever won 11 games and not made the playoffs. We have 11 wins, we better be in the playoffs.

After the game I was talking to my mom about not scoring on a return and I told her that we were being a little more conservative and not trying to hit the home run on every return. Once we got the four returns in a row, coach wanted us to just get the ball up the field. I've been hesitant to do the things I did early in the year because going straight up the field is not my style. I need to start creating something and let my natural instincts take over. I just need to find a happy medium—you cut, you dance—but I need to keep going upfield. It's funny how things work out, because I got the four touchdowns in four games. If I get four touchdowns over the course of an entire season people are going to think that's great. I'm going to think that's great. But now, I had the four and I feel the pressure to do it again. I'm human, I'll admit it. I do feel the pressure. If I don't get the ball at least past midfield, then I feel like I let everyone down. As a team, we're 11-1. But we're not going to be happy unless we win the Super Bowl.

ON TO DENVER

I heard something cool this week. Shania Twain was in Kansas City and she came out on stage wearing my jersey. They must have been sold out of the Priest Holmes and Tony Gonzalez jerseys. I'll have to call and get a photo of her wearing my jersey. I need a picture of that for my locker. But I can't get sidetracked because we're playing Denver Sunday, and I know they're really going to be ticked off.

I've heard some of the things coming out of Denver and I know they remember that return. They're going to be geeked up because I've been fortunate that the last two times I played them I had good games. We've played San Diego and Oakland twice this season and we noticed they come at me differently. They will try to counter something and do some things differently, but we do that, too. All the good teams in the NFL do that.

I know a lot of words are coming out of Denver, from columnists and players, but I don't get into that. Some writer called us frauds. Well, he can say what he wants. We're going to Denver Sunday. We respect them, and I would like to think they respect us.

A Tough Loss

Well, Denver proved they are a good team, and Clinton Portis wore this huge gold (professional wrestling) belt after the game, and I guess he deserved it because he was the champion Sunday afternoon. I guess when you score five touchdowns and rush for 216 yards in a 45-27 victory you can wear whatever you want, no matter how silly it looks.

There was some trash talking going on before that game, but once that game started, it was all business. It was a good game for a half (with Kansas City leading 24-17), then Portis just took it over the second half. It had a playoff game feel. The intensity from the crowd, the players—it all picked up. I thought we played better in some phases of the game than the first time we played them, but we didn't get it done offensively.

We went three and out three straight times in the second half and the defense had to go right back out on the field. We didn't execute. We had some dropped balls—I had a dropped ball—and a couple of mis-throws. Everyone contributed in some way. We went in to look at the film, we saw what we needed to do, and now it's time to go on.

It's kind of weird that even though we lost the game, we still clinched a playoff spot. We haven't been in the playoffs since 1997, so it's a good feeling, but I wish we could have won, and we would have all been feeling a lot better. I know I felt sad and upset at our first meeting because Coach Vermeil got up in front of all of us and took the blame for that loss. That's the type of coach we have. To see him up there all emotional, taking the blame for the loss, that hit my heart. I wish I could go right back out there and make it up to him. I want to reverse that outcome. It's up to us to get the job done.

The loss hurt us in getting home-field advantage, and we wanted to clinch the AFC West title. We didn't do either one, and the fact that we lost at Denver just rubs salt into the wound.

One of my teammates, Larry Johnson, was charged this past week with assault. My first reaction was no way. I wasn't going to pass judgment until I talked to him. He asked coach to speak to the team. He stood up like a man and said he knew he embarrassed the organization, and he assured us that he didn't do it.

Some guys have been in that situation and usually it's not as bad as it seems. It was a big-time stance by a rookie. It was the right thing to do. I believe in him, Coach believes in him, and so do his teammates. That was not a distraction last week. We could use that as an excuse, but we would never do that. Anything that happens during the week goes out the window once the ball is kicked off.

CHAPTER 15

GARY STILLS
on
DANTE HALL

Scott E. Thomas photo

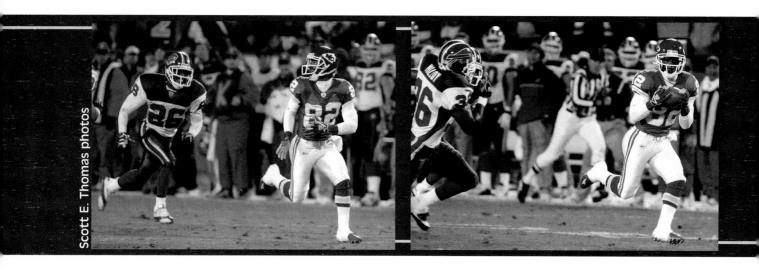

Scott E. Thomas photos

Gary Stills will never sit on a stage with David Letterman, talking about life in the NFL, his favorite rap groups or what it's like playing for Dick Vermeil.

But that doesn't bother the Kansas City Chiefs defensive end/special teams standout.

"We all watched Dante when he was on *Late Show* and he gave us props," Stills said, grinning. "We're not going to get any individual attention, but because of what Dante did this year, we all got recognition. And we won a few games along the way, too."

Stills joined Hall at the Pro Bowl in Hawaii this year, becoming the first non-return member of the Chiefs to ever get such special recognition.

"I think Dante was as excited as I was," said Stills, whose blocking prowess was a big reason for his teammate's success. "Playing on the same special teams unit as Dante makes it special, it was special just being out there with him and being a part of the blocking scheme. It was good to say I was one of the guys out there helping him do his thing."

There was a time when being on a special teams unit was anything but special.

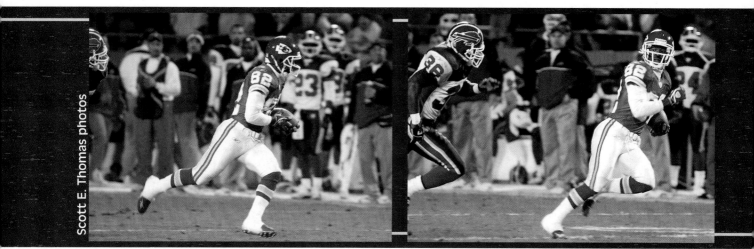

Scott E. Thomas photos

But that all changed when Dick Vermeil became the first special teams coach in the NFL while he was on the staff of the 1969 Los Angeles Rams. Frank Gansz Sr., the father of Kansas City Chiefs special teams coach Frank Gansz Jr., took special teams coaching aspects to new heights when he incorporated Pro Bowl players like Deron Cherry and Albert Lewis into his unit.

Stills, Monte Beisel, Mike Maslowski and other members of the Chiefs special team unit are making their own headlines, thanks in part to the success of Hall.

"I think it's easier on you when you have a great player like Dante," Still said. "He makes it easy when he has the ability to take it all the way every time he touches the ball.

"There was some pressure when he was trying to get No. 5 (which came in a post-season loss to Indianapolis). The pressure came when we all tried to get him the record. Pressure comes when the adrenaline starts flowing, and it was flowing every time he touched the ball after he had the four touchdowns in four games. We all wanted to get him No. 5. It didn't happen this year (in the regular season), but we're all going for it next year."

Scott E. Thomas photos

Stills said the excitement created by the special teams unit this year is something he'll never forget. But don't ask him to try to guess what's going on in Dante's head as he's about to field a punt or kick.

"I don't know what's going on with Dante," Still said, grinning. "He sees a lot more than I see out there, because everything is in front of him. He can make things happen. In that Denver Broncos game, I'm watching him make a move, and make another move and he's gone. He can make a lot of people miss.

"We had the red cape and the bull in the Houston game (on Hall's second return

for a touchdown) because he's coming up, and if I don't see him, he runs into me and that play doesn't even happen. I jumped up in the air, he runs under me and takes it to the house."

While he can't promise a touchdown on every return, Stills can promise an all-out effort by every member of the team. "It's very, very important to do what's in the scheme, but it's difficult sometimes because Dante's out there being Dante and doing what he does best," Stills said. "He makes so many moves you don't know where he's at. You can get caught turning around looking for him. Half the time, the crowd will tell you where he's

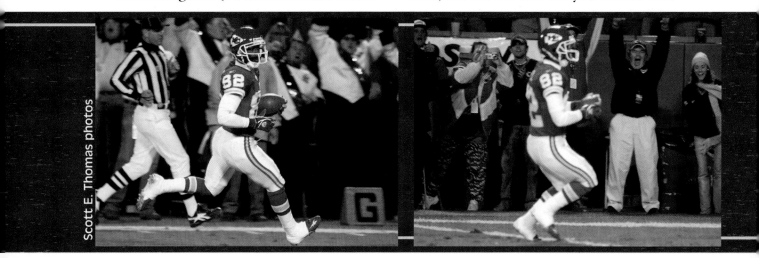

Scott E. Thomas photos

at or if he took it to the house or if he's down. That's how you can get caught up in finding where he is."

The roar of the crowd at Arrowhead gets Stills pumped. He believes the energy created by 78,000 screaming fans impacted many of Hall's returns.

"You hear the crowd, and you're anticipating the same thing they are," Stills said. "You know that it might happen. It's happened in four games in a row, but the special thing about it is that you're out on the field blocking and helping him get that touchdown. "Our special teams

group is really special. I think we're getting as much recognition as the offense or the defense. We want to help the offense get the ball on the 40 or beyond. We can make or break a game. We have so much confidence in each other, and that's a big reason for the success. I know the offense can score any time, any place. But when we give them the ball in good field condition, you can feel the confidence level of every player grow.

"And when you're out there with Dante, you know something good is going to happen—you can just feel it."

"ONCE HE BREAKS OUT, IT'S A DONE DEAL."
—Frank Bush, Denver special teams coach

16

DEAR DIARY: WE ARE THE CHAMPIONS!

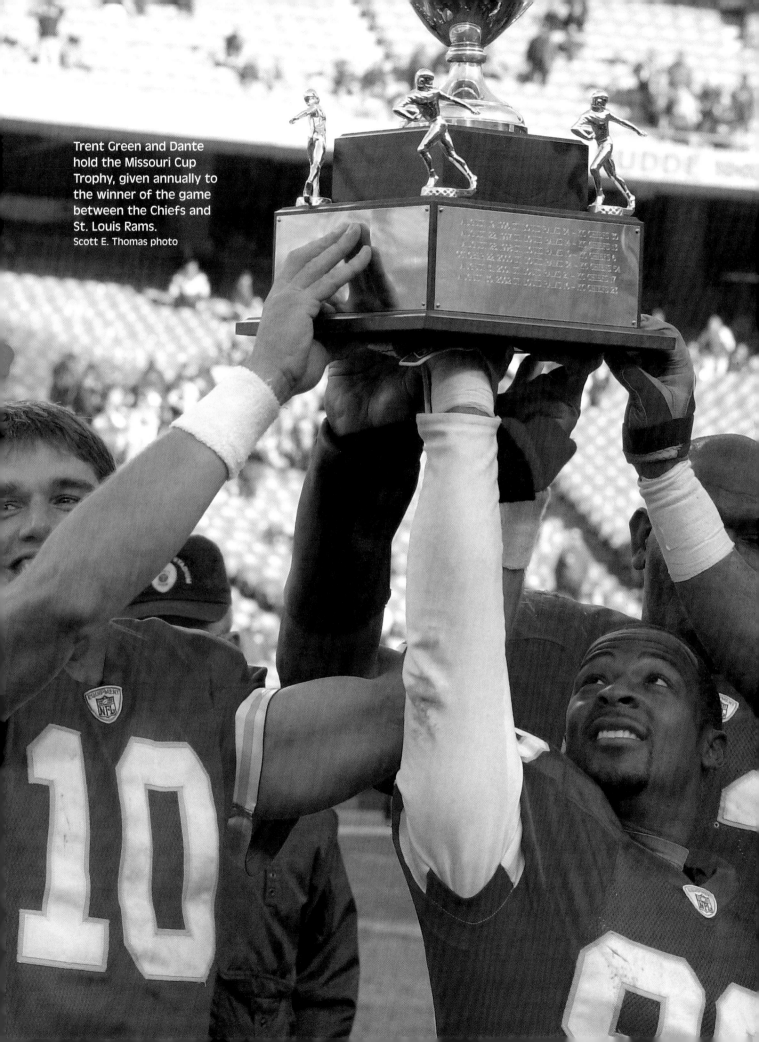

Trent Green and Dante hold the Missouri Cup Trophy, given annually to the winner of the game between the Chiefs and St. Louis Rams.
Scott E. Thomas photo

Does anything compare with winning a championship? I don't think so! Our ultimate goal this year is the Super Bowl, but Sunday we won the AFC West championship with a 45-17 win over the Lions. And oh, it was so, so sweet. We got our championship hats in the locker room, our T-shirts—it was a great day. I am very proud. That was one of the goals—we're just going right down the goal sheet.

I even became a fan on the sideline watching some of the plays Al was calling, the passes Trent was making—the things Priest and Tony were doing. This was the offensive game we'd been waiting for all season.

I knew we were going to be aggressive this week. We had signs on our locker room stools—MAKE A PLAY—so I knew we'd be aggressive. We wanted to score as many points as we could.

Priest scored a couple of touchdowns and has 22 on the season. He's going after Marshall Faulk's single-season record of 25 and I have a ringside seat to it all. Watching him is like watching Superman. He does things on the field you can't believe. He's not a mere mortal. I think he's MVP of the league. He's such a great part of our offense. There aren't enough words to describe this guy. He's a smart runner, he's patient—by that, I mean he waits for the holes to open—he's smart, he can catch a pass out of the backfield, he can dive over the top. He can get it done so many ways. He's kind of quiet, but I know he's close to his offensive line. They take care of him and he takes care of them. To go out and get a performance like the one we got was unbelievable.

And speaking of unbelievable, I thought I had No. 5 against the Lions—and so did all the fans at Arrowhead. Looking back at the film, Gary Stills didn't need to stay on the kicker, he just needed to stay on the guy he was blocking. What happened was, when the kicker came over, they cut my sideline angle, and I couldn't come back because of the pursuit from the backside. And please, let me say something. First of all, just because a player is a kicker, it doesn't mean he's not a good athlete. I mean look at Jason Baker, our kicker. He's laid some hats on some returns this year.

If you look at highlights, the kickers are making some plays. There are a few, here and there, who don't want to tackle. But most of them are athletes. People in this league are so fast. I had to pause a little bit when I saw the kicker, and that was enough to allow the backside pursuit to catch me. It's nobody's fault. This is the NFL and it's full of great athletes. Plus, blocking is hard! It's hard enough when I try to block for Priest, it's hard to say what should or shouldn't be done.

And I have to make another point. I caught a punt in that game that I should probably have waved off. I got hit by two Lions, and wow—I mean, I got hit. It was the first time in my career that I started bleeding. My nose was bleeding, and it's still sore today. I need to leave that doggone ball alone. I took one for the team. I thought I had the fifth TD, but we have two more games, so we'll see what happens.

One other thing that really pleased me was that my boy from Texas, Derrick Blaylock, had a great game. He caught that 63-yard pass from Trent and took it

Dante and tight end Jason Dunn check out the action on the field.

to the house. He finished with 100 yards in the air and that just makes me so happy because he works his butt off in practice and now he's getting rewarded for that. He's playing behind Priest and Larry, but his hard work is paying off. I was watching him break tackles and I thought, "Wow! Blaylock, where did that come from?"

We can appreciate this win, but now it's time to think about our next opponent, the Minnesota Vikings. I don't like playing on turf, I like the natural grass, but we need to win to get homefield advantage, so this is a big one. But in the NFL, they're all big.

CHAPTER 17

KEN RUCKER
on
DANTE HALL

Stephen Dunn/Getty Images

Ken Rucker knows a good thing when he sees it.

The former running backs coach at Texas A&M also knows a thing or two about Texas tall tales. He'd heard about an extraordinary running back at Nimitz High School, but didn't really believe the Aggies had a shot at recruiting him.

"All the big schools wanted Dante Hall," said Rucker, the former A&M running back coach. "He was outstanding. You know, he was explosive, he could make you miss, he had the quickness and speed to take it to the house. He was a real talent."

Rucker wasn't asked to initially recruit Dante. Larry Slade, who is now the defensive backs coach at Tennessee, was the man assigned to get Dante's name on the dotted line of a national letter of intent.

"Coach Slade was the recruiter for Dante, but I made a visit when he went to Dante's home," Rucker said. "We sat down and talked and got to know one another. I think I was more impressed with him as a person than I was as a player. And his mother is a wonderful woman. You could tell that she was a major influence in his life.

"Then I visited him at Nimitz and I felt like this was a great young man who would mean a lot to our program. Everyone loved him. He had such a great personality and strong character.

"When I worked on Fisher DeBerry's staff at Air Force in 1984, we had a young man by the name of Anthony Roberson.

He is now an L-16 pilot stationed in Europe. Dante reminded me of him. He's not the biggest back around, but he was so explosive. Anthony played running back and in high school, and Dante was a great running back and a great blocker. I told him, 'You're another Anthony Roberson.'"

Rucker dreamed of signing Dante, and that dream became a reality when many of the big schools backed off after his injury-plagued senior year in high school. Because of his affection for Rucker and the fact that the university was close to his family, Dante signed with A&M.

You could say he immediately was in Rucker's doghouse. But at A&M, that's a good thing.

"I nicknamed him Pup," Rucker said, laughing at the special memory. "When I called him that, Dante just smiled this big ol' smile. You could tell he liked the nickname."

Dante liked it so much he went out and got PUP tattooed on his bicep.

"When he came to our program, he was just a pup, a yearling. It took a few games, but he made such a great impact as a true freshman. He was a baby among the backs, just a pup. He was bright eyed and bushy tailed and wanted to learn. I still love him to death. As a coach, you treat every player the same, but it's the way he responds that makes him special. He knew I cared about him going to class. I wasn't trying to substitute for his father, but I was like his surrogate dad and he never wanted to let me down.

A familiar sight for Aggies fans—Dante scoring another touchdown.
Brian Bahr/Getty Images

And he didn't. He wanted to please. That's the type of relationship we have. We might not talk for months, but when we do, it's like we just saw each other. Now, that's a special relationship.

When Dante arrived at A&M, the school already featured "The Three Horsemen," running backs Sirr Parker, Eric Bernard and Tiki Hardeman.

"We had three great backs Dante's freshman year. Did you know that each of them, including Dante, rushed for 500-plus yards his first year? I knew it was going to be a great season because we'd played Michigan in the Alamo Bowl the year before Dante arrived and beat them with those three kids when they were true freshmen.

"The next year we signed Dante—you think that wasn't exciting to this ol' running back coach? Those guys were good for Dante. On his recruiting visit, they got to know each other. Sirr and Tiki were his hosts, and I'm sure they showed him a good time and got to know him real well. When he came on campus, he fit right in and he knew he didn't have to produce right away because we already had three pretty darned good backs. He didn't have the pressure, and he was a kickoff specialist and it was great for him and great for the Aggies."

While Dante enjoyed a successful freshman campaign, the waters were not always smooth. Even when he and Rucker butted heads, both men knew their relationship would always remain strong.

"I loved him then," Rucker said, "and it hurt me to get on him at times. He was just a young man trying to get better. He gave me everything he had. We had a great rapport."

Rucker looked on from the sidelines like a proud father as Dante began to make a name for himself on the collegiate level.

"As a freshman, he was a leader. God got up one day and felt like creating Dante Hall. And the bottom line is, he lives up to everything that God created him to be. We were playing San Diego State at home and he had a great kickoff return against them. He set them up, made them miss and took it a long distance. I can remember that game so vividly. We went up and played Colorado.

"They always have a great run defense, so our goal was to try and reach 150 yards on the ground. We rushed for almost 300 yards with Dante and Sirr at tailback. We moved Tiki to fullback. We ran off tackle and went weak with the tall sweep and hung our hat on those two guys running the ball. It was an ABC-TV game and it was just great."

Rucker coached Dante for three years, before an illness in the family forced the popular coach to move to Chapel Hill, North Carolina.

"I had a sick dad in 1998 and that caused me to uproot and go to Chapel Hill," Rucker said. "My dad was 86 years young and dying of cancer and I needed to get back there and get closer to him, so I missed Dante's senior year. I missed coaching him. We had such a great relationship. Sometimes I had to give him tough love. But he always knew where I was coming from."

And still does.

Dante calls Rucker " . . . one of the most special people in my life."

"I'm so humbled by that," Rucker said. "That touches me. When I think of Dante, I think of a special person, and a spectacular player. You couldn't hem him up in a 5x5 room. He'd take it the distance and just be smiling."

Whether it was on the football field or in the Rucker home, coach and player developed a bond that could not be broken.

"We'd have occasional meals at the house," Rucker said. "My wife, Nancy, would cook for him. I coached him tough at work and he saw a different side of me at home. We worked our players hard, but I loved 'em and hugged 'em up. I wanted them to know how special they were to me when they were playing, and how special they are to me today."

On any given Sunday, Rucker can be found near a television set, tuning into Chiefs games.

"I try to follow all my guys who make it to the pros," he said, "but with Dante, it's a little bit easier. After I finish my coaching responsibilities on a Sunday, I'll tune into a game, and there's Dante with his X-Factor Gatorade. Or I might tune in late at night and there's Dante on the David Letterman television program.

"He's such a personable young man, with a great smile and personality. He's a talented guy who has stood firm with his faith and has honored God through it all. I just know that God has a plan for him, a very special play.

"Jeremiah 29:11 says, 'God has a plan for you. One to help you, not to harm you. One to make you prosper.' Dante is living up to that tenfold."

"BLOCKING FOR DANTE ON SPECIAL TEAMS IS EASY, IT'S EXCITING. YOU NEVER KNOW IF YOUR BLOCK IS THE ONE THAT'S GOING TO HELP HIM GO ALL THE WAY. HE GETS US ALL PUMPED UP."

—Donald Willis, Kansas City Chiefs special teams wedge blocker

CHAPTER

18

DEAR DIARY:
A NIGHTMARE
IN MINNESOTA

Dante prepares to return a kick against Minnesota.
Scott E. Thomas photo

I wish I knew what to say, but I don't. You go to another team's stadium, play hard, really mix it up with them, and maybe—just maybe—you can live with a loss in the 16th week of the season. But to go in and get your butt whipped in every phase of the game—offense, defense and special teams—that's just unacceptable. To make matters worse, I had to leave the game because my right calf muscle started to cramp. I thought I was going into a full-body cramp. Was it the turf? Did I need to be more hydrated? I don't know.

Now, the question keeps coming up: You lost three of your last four on the road. Which was the toughest? They were all tough, but Minnesota was the toughest. There was so much hype around the game, they jumped out to the big lead and it went downhill. They jumped on us early, took Priest out of the game, and it was over before it got started.

I keep asking myself how that can happen when all the games are so important. But I know I'm not the only guy on the team asking that question. We knew the game would be faster because of the turf, but we didn't think it would turn out like it did.

We got behind and we tried to come back and we couldn't. We had several chances to get back in the game and we didn't allow ourselves to do it. But it won't happen again—no one is going to dominate us like that. We went from a game where we scored touchdowns on seven of eight possessions to a game where we couldn't do anything until it's too late. It happens. You don't like it to happen, but it does. We got outplayed,

and that is one of the things I am beginning to realize.

On any given day, you can get beat or you can beat anyone. You have to execute, and we didn't. But much like the loss at Denver where we clinched the playoff spot, we got a playoff bye despite losing at Minnesota. You have to take the good with the bad, even though you don't want to. We have to learn from this.

It was well documented that (defensive linemen) Eric Hicks and Ryan Sims got into an argument after the game. It happened in front of the media and everyone, and people started saying the team is crumbling and falling apart. That's not true. It's absolutely not true. They were both PO'd, and they should be PO'd because we didn't play well. Are you happy after you get embarrassed like that? If you are, you better find another profession.

That was an isolated incident, and those guys chose to handle it that way. Now, they need to take that anger and that frustration out on the field when we play Chicago in the last game of the regular season. You get your butt whipped, you better want to make your next opponent pay for it. After it happened, I got up from my locker and said, "Okay, time for everyone to go!" I was trying to lighten the situation.

We don't want to forget about the loss at Minnesota, but we can't let it affect our preparation for the Bears game. We need to correct the mistakes and then go out and win the last game to get some momentum going into the postseason. We can play better and we can execute bet-

ter. We have one game left before the playoffs. We've had some bumps in the road the past few weeks, but it's nothing we can't fix.

If something needs to be fixed, we have the master repairman in Coach Vermeil. I love the guy because he doesn't come in and point fingers and blame certain indi-

viduals. He knows that happens. He doesn't like it. He tips his hat to those guys and we go on. You're not going to see any finger-pointing or name calling. Not on a team Dick Vermeil coaches. Confidence is everything in this league and we need to go out and really play well against Chicago and build some confidence going into the playoffs.

137

CHAPTER 19

LYLE WEST
on
DANTE HALL

Dante leads the Chiefs to another victory.
Scott E. Thomas photo

Lyle West dreams of being a starter in the National Football League. But right now, the Kansas City Chiefs defensive back enjoys his dream job as one of the members of the team's special teams unit.

"I think guys who take pride in special teams are few and far between," West said. "A lot of guys have aspirations of starting, and that's all they think about. But when you affect the game like we have, it makes it special. And when you have a guy like Dante back there, it just makes it so much fun."

Following a Dante Hall return for a touchdown, West eagerly anticipates the Monday morning meetings in which all phases of the special teams game are dissected. "On Monday morning, we watch film and each guy gets to see how he contributed," West said, "although Dante does most of it by himself, it's just fun. I feel honored to be a part of our special teams.

"You'll be blocking your guy and you'll feel the play is over and then you hear the crowd erupt and you're trying to get a block and try not to get in his way because you know he can do something special. You don't want to clog a hole and keep him from doing his thing out there."

Dante has become famous around the league for his helter-skelter runs in which it appears that he's making moves up as the play unfolds.

"There is definitely a scheme to it," West said, "I guess you could call it controlled chaos. We have a scheme, and 85 to 90 percent of the time he takes where it's supposed to go. But like in the Denver game, it was all him. None of us could say we really contributed on that touchdown because there was nothing there—it was all him. I would have to say it was the most impressive football play I've ever seen. A lot of guys do good things on other runs, but it doesn't take a lot to spring him."

And an appreciative Arrowhead Stadium crowd energizes the special team players as they approach the field.

"I can't help but get excited when I line up on the kickoff return team and the

Scott E. Thomas photos

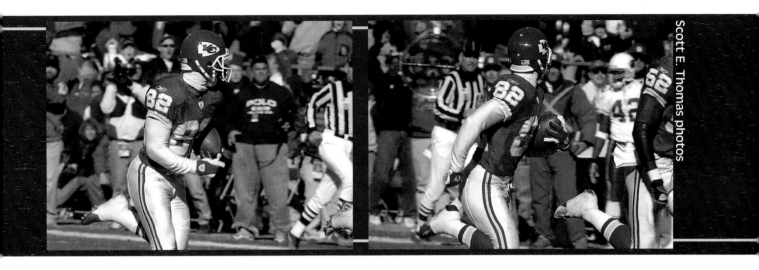

crowd starts getting excited. You pick up that buzz and you get more and more excited. That raises your intensity level. It's awesome."

West was a part of all four of Dante's regular-season returns for touchdowns. And he believes it will take some time before he appreciates the impact that record-tying performance will have on his life.

"Will I totally understand what I've been a part of?" he asks himself. "No. Will I understand in 10 or 15 years? Probably. Right now, it's just hard to imagine being a part of something like four in a row. I may never truly know what Dante and we as a team have accomplished. I take pride in him going to the Pro Bowl. When I look and see that I lead the team in blocks, and I see Dante going out of his way to congratulate and thank the other guys on the special teams, it just makes me feel good, like we're getting it done as a team."

As West talks about Dante, a group of reporters surround the top return man in the game's locker to talk about next week's opponent. Dante answers the questions with great care.

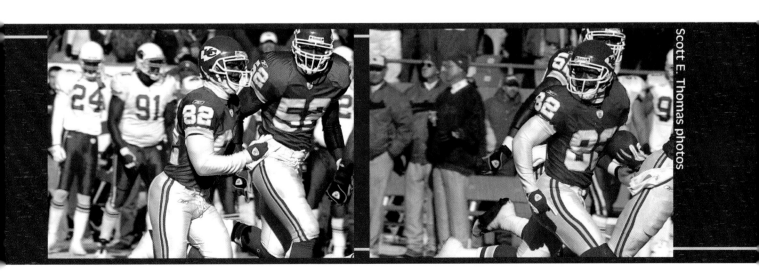

"I have been very impressed with how Dante has handled his success. Take any other guy—you get all this attention, you go on Letterman, and you are bound to change. But not Dante. He has done a great job with his success. I haven't seen him change at all. I've seen success change guys, and I'm talking about guys who haven't done nearly as much as Dante. When you see a guy like Dante and see how he handles all this attention, it just makes you appreciate him even more."

West pauses, and adds, "This is a part of his life he will never forget, and he wants everyone to enjoy it. He's always talking about his mother and her influence and the influence God has in his life. He loves to go home and have some home cooking. I think about that and use it in perspective for my life. When I'm gone, are they going to talk about the kind of car I was driving—no. Are they going to talk about what type of father I was, what type of man I was—absolutely. And that's how I feel about Dante. He's a great athlete, but he's an even better individual. He's so nice, so down to earth, that's how I'm going to remember him."

So what does it take to make it as a special teams player in the NFL?

"Special teams is an attitude," West said, emphatically. "There are guys out there who are bigger and stronger than me, so what's the difference? We just want to get the job done. We work on techniques and want to know other teams' tendencies. Does the other guy like to run over you or around you? I'd love to be a starter, but I will always take a lot of pride in helping Dante accomplish what he did this season.

"Whatever it takes, we'll do it. Whatever Coach (Frank) Gansz wants me to do, I'll do it. Coach Vermeil paid me a great compliment last week when he said we take guys like Lyle West for granted. They just go out and do their jobs and we expect them to do their jobs. You don't draw any attention to yourself, you just do your job.

"That means a lot to me. A guy like me is quiet, and everyone needs a pat on the back once in a while, I appreciate that. I just go out there and think of every play as if I don't make my block, Dante's not going to go all the way. The worst feeling in the world is when your guy makes the tackle. I don't want that to happen. I punch in, work my butt off. When I punch out, I go home and enjoy my family."

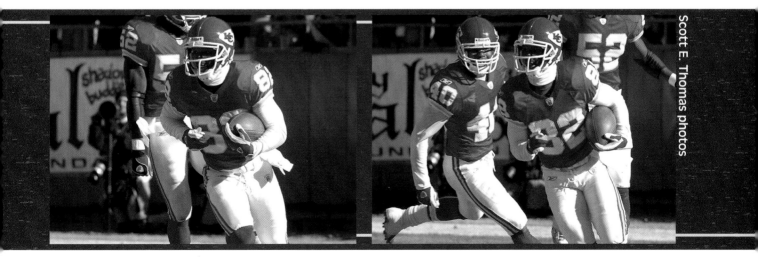

20

DEAR DIARY: ON TO THE PLAYOFFS

Scott E. Thomas photo

Who said 13 is unlucky? I can assure you that it wasn't a member of the 13-3 Kansas City Chiefs. I didn't get my fifth touchdown from Santa, but we got a 31-3 season-ending victory over the Chicago Bears and a week off before we start the playoffs, so I'm feeling pretty good. I'm beat up and bumped knees with one of their linebackers so my knee is swollen, but it will be fine and I will be ready for the playoffs.

We're going to work out this week and Saturday we will practice, take Sunday and Monday off and come back Tuesday and get ready for our opponent. I'm sore and have a little shoulder problem, so I'll take care of myself. It's really positive to get everyone healthy. I am so excited about the playoffs. We've played some games that had a playoff atmosphere, and I am happy we can give the fans of Kansas City a playoff game.

The game Sunday didn't really mean a lot because we were locked into the No. 2 playoff spot. We didn't play for a playoff position but we wanted to end the season strong, get a win and get our confidence back. Minnesota had put a good whuppin' on us and we needed to play well against the Bears. And everyone on the team wanted Priest to get the NFL single-season rushing record. He needed two touchdowns and Tony (Richardson) and the guys on the line wanted to do everything they could to get him that record. And I know it meant a lot to Priest, too.

When you think of all the great backs to play the game, it's pretty impressive to see Priest get the record. And we can all share the record. I told Priest that if I got a long pass, I was going to take it to the goal line and step out of bounds and let him do the rest. I didn't need a touchdown on offense. I needed one on special teams. I'm so happy for Priest. I know I didn't get No. 5, but what a great, great season. I'm going to get No. 5 in the playoffs and hopefully it will help us beat our opponent.

Our return game was strong against the Bears. My first return went 44 yards and once again, I thought I was gone. I hit the sideline and started kicking. I saw a blocker upfield and made the kicker miss, then I felt someone hit me from the back. Darn it. But we had good field position so I had some satisfaction. That was my longest return, but my first punt return was my best chance to score.

I watched film today and it was like so many other returns. It was set up to go all the way. I needed to make that last guy miss. It's tough to swallow. I would be telling you a bold-faced lie if I didn't say I was disappointed I didn't get the record by myself. But it's over with and now all I'm focusing on is the playoffs.

Now, we just have to see who we play. We have a little motto where we say we're the only team that can beat us at Arrowhead. We've won 13 in a row at home and don't want to see that streak come to an end.

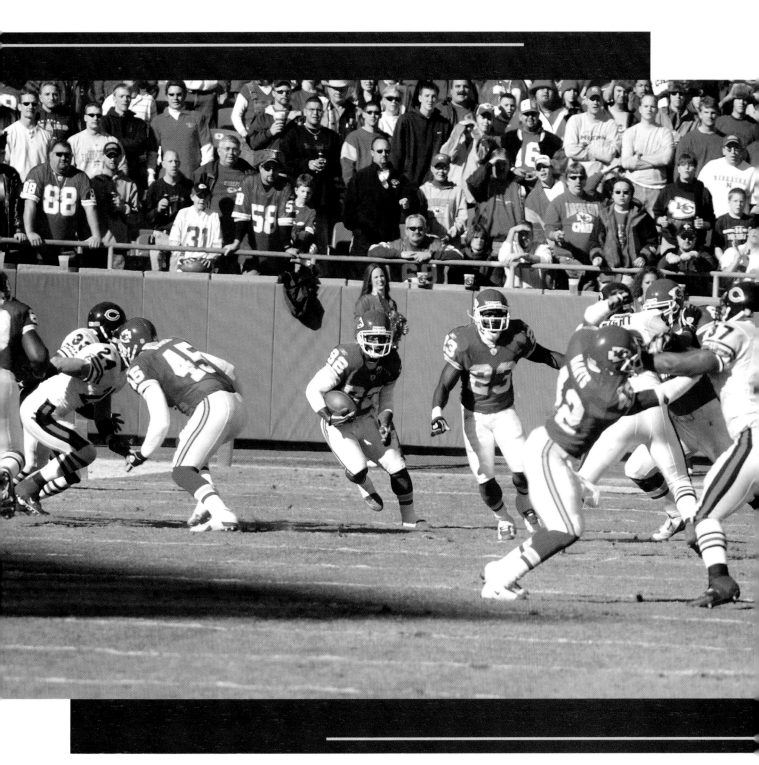

With a hole like that to run through, it's easy to see why
Dante lavishes so much praise on his teammates.
Scott E. Thomas photo

DEAR DIARY:
I GOT NO. 5—BUT I'D
TRADE IT FOR A WIN

Scott E. Thomas photo

My dream came true. I got No. 5—but it just leaves me with a hollow feeling, an empty feeling, when it doesn't result in a victory. I took one 92 yards and it was a middle wedge. They were overloading to the right all game, but we were trying to bring it back to the left. On that particular return, we had a middle wedge, which gave me the opportunity to take it up the middle and go to the right or the left. I pretty much did all of that. I took it left, then cut it back right. I saw a lane and made it through the first wave. I wasn't worried about getting caught from behind because I didn't have to cut back to the pursuit. On that play, once I hit the lane, not even the kicker was in sight. I felt safe. A lot of people made good blocks, everybody did a good job.

We were down by 14 and I was thinking that we needed a return. We were running out of time. Frank Gansz Jr. came up to me and said, "That's what I'm talking about. That's what I'm talking about!" It got the crowd fired up and the team fired up. I've never played in front of a crowd where it was that loud. NEVER! You talk about teams picking it up in the postseason, well, our fans picked it up, too. They were into the game. I feel so bad that they had to leave after we lost. I thought the return would be enough to swing the momentum back our way, but Peyton wouldn't have anything to do with it. He was just unstoppable.

I finished that game with 208 kickoff return yards. That's a Chiefs single-game postseason record and the third highest total in NFL history. So can someone please tell me why I feel so bad? I still feel like crying. We made the plays, but we didn't make enough plays. I was lucky to get a touchdown reception, too. We scored 31 points. They scored 38. That's the story of the game. I was hoping to be an impact player, and I was. We made the big plays, they just made more than we did.

The loss is sad—so sad. But there were so many good things about this season. I finally got involved in the offense and felt like I was really a part of it. From working with (receivers coach) Charlie Joiner, I feel comfortable as a wide receiver. I was a running back in college, and that's quite a change. But I finally got to the point where I could just react out there and not have to think about running my routes and things like that. I want to get to the point where Trent will feel like if he hits me in the hands, it's a sure catch. Maybe I can go from the X-Factor to the Sure Thing.

I'm not going to point a finger at my defense. I'm tipping my hat to Peyton Manning. It was so impressive to watch him give all his backs and wide receivers their routes and responsibilities. Then he goes back and throws a perfect pass. How do you do that? It's not of this earth. That's not human. I couldn't hear myself think on the sidelines. It was a sad end to a great season. We're all going to remember that loss and use it as motivation for the future.

Scott E. Thomas photo

CHAPTER 22

DEAR DIARY: I MET OUR COUNTRY'S REAL HEROES

Here are our nation's real heroes—the
men and women of the armed forces.
Scott E. Thomas photo

For the second year in a row I was selected to represent the Kansas City Chiefs at the Pro Bowl. I feel lucky and blessed to be picked. And if I am lucky and blessed and picked to go to it next year, I will. But as far as the game goes, I hate it. I know that might sound harsh, but that's how I feel. Right now is the time I'm supposed to be getting my body back in shape, and my ribs hurt and I'm sore and it's all because of playing in that game.

I'm getting some treatment and I want to be ready and 100 percent for the Kansas City Chiefs. I can't do anything. I can't sleep. If I'm blessed and able to go again, I will. But it's tough, because you have nothing but superstars out there trying to run you down. It's dangerous out there, especially for a guy my size. You can take a beating out there, and I did this year. Now, I've got two months of pain, and after I get done dealing with this pain, I've got to start dealing with off-season conditioning. I'm not too high on the Pro Bowl. It's a great honor, but it's more work than pleasure.

While I might not have enjoyed this year's game, I hope the group of Chiefs personnel and players we took did. (Pro Bowl lineman) Will Shields set everything up, all I did was pay my little part. We got a charter, and anyone from the team who wanted to go to the game was able to go. The pro bowlers split up the cost. I flew over on my own, though, because I flew to Hawaii from Houston. Some parts of the week are fun. The activities are fun, you get to meet all the players and get their opinions.

But the one thing I will remember the rest of my life had nothing to do with the game or the activities surrounding the game. I visited the 205th Infantry. It was awesome. I got to go out and see a trial run of what they were going to do before they went to Iraq.

You know how people come to see us practice? Well, we went to see them practice for something that's a whole lot more important than a football game. It was unreal. Oh man, heavy artillery. They let us shoot the guns and everything…M-16s and M somethings, a lot of M's. We weren't in combat gear, we just wore our regular clothes, but we were out in the Hawaiian woods. It was just unbelievable to see how they prepare for fighting for our country. These people are the real heroes. We're not heroes, we're just football players, we play a game. They fight for their country and are willing to give their lives for their country.

I kept thinking how we're at war, and so many people call football a war. Believe me, football is not a war. I didn't need to go out and see those military drills to know how important those folks are to our freedom and our country. I already knew that. They are the true heroes, and I salute all of them. I know that this is a different type of war. We put our bodies on the line. They put their lives on the line—and there is a big difference. I guarantee you a lot of tough guys in the NFL wouldn't be so tough if it came to putting their lives on the line. The men and women of the military are the heroes. We're entertainers.

Just imagine putting your life on the line for your job. I have so much respect for them. If I had a chance of dying, I'd find another field of business. We're no heroes, man.

CHAPTER

23

DEAR DIARY: LOOKING BACK

Looking back on a great season.
Scott E. Thomas photo

Wow, has it really been two and a half months since the season ended? It seems like it ended yesterday, but it also seems like it ended a year ago. We had so many successes but failed to reach that ultimate goal.

I've just come back from the indoor practice facility and my first team workout since the season ended. It felt good to see the guys, find out what they had been up to and get back into a routine.

People are always asking me, whether I'm in Kansas City, back home in Houston, or in Hawaii—they want to know if I can appreciate all the good things that happened this season.

Absolutely!

I can't believe all the opportunities I've had. And what I really can't believe are all the opportunities I've had to turn down. I had to turn down ESPN, because they wanted me to be on a game show. The Country Music Television (CMT) awards show just called and wanted me to be a presenter, and I can't do it because I'm committed to doing this thing for the NFL Network. Week in and week out there are opportunities, so wow, I must have had a helluva season.

It's wild to look back on the last year and think about the things I've done and the people I've met. I enjoy it because of the experiences. You name a city, and nine times out of 10 I've been there. The only drawback is I'm a homebody. I'm a guy who grew up in Houston and didn't really know if I could play college ball, let alone in the NFL. Now, people ask me to

come to their town, they send a limo and a chauffeur and do it up right.

As I sit in the Arrowhead Stadium parking lot, my mind is spinning. It's overwhelming. I'm not used to being this busy. In the previous three years, this was the time of year I just hung out with my friends and family and chilled. Now, I feel like a businessman. I'm not P. Diddy, Carl Peterson or Donald Trump—I can only imagine their lifestyles. I don't want them. I don't even have time to see my own family. The last time I saw my uncle I had two cell phones going, had to hit the computer to check my e-mail and had a cab waiting for me in the driveway. Man, it's just been that crazy.

But it's not going to keep on like this—no way! There are a lot of things I want to do, but I'm shutting it down in May. I want to have an even better season in 2004 than I did last year. And to do that, I have to say no to everyone and get back to work. I'm looking forward to getting back to work, because then I'll have a steady routine I can follow and things won't be so crazy.

But don't get me wrong. My off season might have been crazy, but it was a lot of fun. I did a lot of traveling, for business and pleasure, worked on my house—landscaping, pool, painting, things like that. And, of course, spent as much time as possible with Adonis.

I look at my calendar and see the season ended January 11, and I figured out since that date, I have not spent one full week in Houston. I have not had seven straight days at home. I just went to Hawaii for

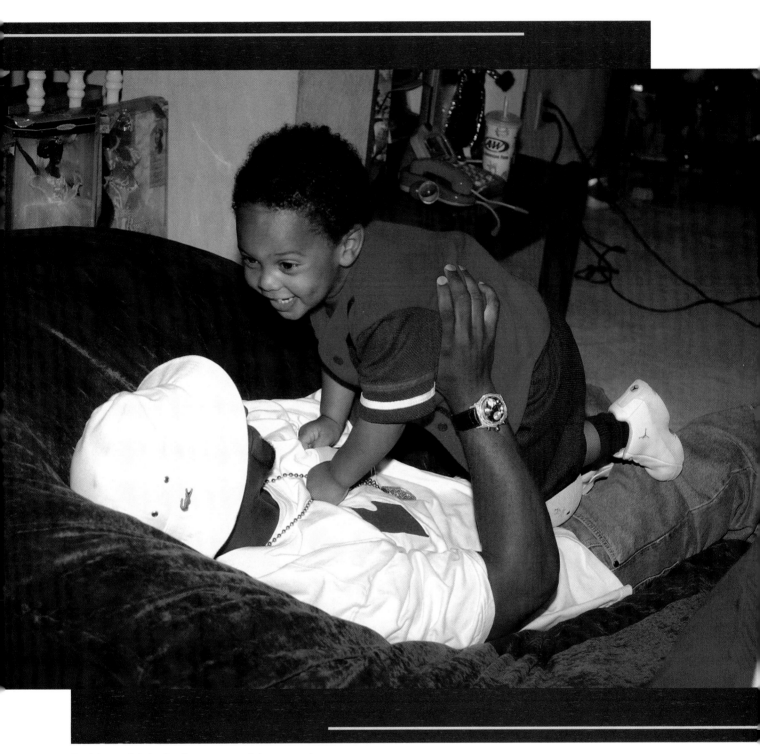

Daddy and Adonis share a special moment.
Scott E. Thomas photo

the Coor's Light convention. It's a tough job, but someone has to do it. At the convention they have the Coor's Light twins and that helped make it one of the rare appearances where you have fun and get paid.

Brazil was a pleasure trip. Every year the past two or three years I pick a city I want to visit and this year it was Rio de Janero for Carnivale. Oh, it was so awesome. I met (director) John Singleton, and we hung out and had a great time, but I doubt if I'm in his next film. I was there four days and three nights and I had my picture taken in front of that huge statue of Christ. My college roommate and I went. He's my travel partner. It's neat to share my success. I'm not a selfish dude. I bought my mom her house, first, but I also want my friends to travel with me. I don't want them to just hear about it.

While Hawaii and Rio were fun, I had to go to Chicago to film a commercial. The end result is great, because it's for the new drink, Gatorade X-Factor. Have you seen it? There are some clips of me running the ball and then all these shots of athletes making the X-Factor sign. And it ends with me looking at the camera and these two beads of sweat rolling down my forehead, making the X-Factor sign.

How long does it last? About two seconds. That took two or three hours to get. Can you believe it? They kept pouring the water to get the X to cross at the same time and at the right place. I had to bring my head up right. They marked something, then poured water on my head, but I love that commercial.

It wasn't as much fun to make as the one for the NFL playoffs with Don Cheadle. He's one of the guys I've been fortunate enough to meet who is real, a real solid person. He reminds me of Dick Vermeil. He just e-mailed me and said he wants to hang out. How cool is that? Denzel Washington and Al Pacino are my favorite actors, but they better watch out, because Don Cheadle is moving up.

When I meet people like Don Cheadle, or when David Letterman asks me to be his guest, I just can't believe it. But I'm beginning to believe it. I didn't realize until I did this piece for the NFL Network that people like LeBron James, Allen Iverson—people I put way up there—look at me and know about the X-Factor. Every time I turn on the tube I want to see LeBron dunk on someone and I want to see AI go for 40. And I realize it's kind of the same. They want to see me take one to the house. They want to see me shake the shoes off somebody. It's not about expectations. It's about the responsibility to entertain.

It's crazy. When I flip it like that, it's big—really, really big. I refuse to be a flop. That was my motivation last year—I had the Pro Bowl year in 2002 and I wanted to follow it up with a Pro Bowl year in 2003. Then, I got four in a row and everyone was going crazy. Then, I went 11 weeks without taking one to the house. I want to get to a point where I get it done year in and year out.

I know Coach Vermeil and some other people are saying I can't say no. Well, I want them to know it all depends how you look at it. You can take this avenue and be an a-hole, or you can look at it like, I got $50,000 for doing this. And someone says, 'You could have gotten $100,000.' Well, I could have gotten nothing, too. So I'm happy for whatever comes my way. I'm not a greedy person. I'm just happy to have an opportunity.

There is so much more that I want to do. I'm probably going to be done with football when I'm 30. Then, I can start thinking about making money. I want to deal in real estate and so many other things. I'm going to have plenty of time to make money. Now, it's about the opportunity. When I'm out of football, no one is going to care if I was in a Gatorade commercial, or running on a football field with Don Cheadle or sitting up there on stage with David Letterman. You can't take that away from me. It is hard for me to say no right now.

Although I enjoy looking back on 2003, I'm ready to start preparing for 2004. I'm looking at this season like I'm going to get five (touchdowns). That's that. I'm not being cocky or anything, that's just how I feel. That's my goal. I know there are going to be some high expectations, but no one has any higher expectations than I do for myself. Every time I see anyone who wants to talk about football, or watch game film, all they want to talk about are the returns. How could I get four in week five and not get one in 11 games and then get one in the postseason? Can someone please explain that to me? Then, I see where Priest gets his jersey and shoes retired in Canton (at the Pro Football Hall of Fame) from his record touchdowns, and I think that should be Priest and Dante. I want to see my jersey retired and hanging in Canton. That's a personal goal of mine.

And I'm going to make it happen.

"EVEN IF I HIT A 50-YARDER WITH 5.0 (SECONDS OF HANGTIME). THAT'S STILL A LONG TIME FOR GUYS TO COVER AND GIVES HIM A LITTLE BIT OF ROOM. IF YOU GIVE THIS GUY FIVE YARDS, THAT'S FIVE YARDS TOO MUCH."
—Josh Bidwell, Green Bay Packers punter

CHAPTER 24

CHILDREN'S LETTERS TO DANTE

Dear Dante Hall
I ♥ Fotball I ♥ you Dante
Hall I whis they wolud
loct grils play
Football.

Frum Laurey
2 erad

ome of Dante Hall's biggest fans are the smallest people in the stadium. "I think kids like me so much because I'm not much bigger than them," Dante says with a smile. While Dante can't answer every letter sent to him at Arrowhead Stadium, he enjoys reading them. Here are some of his favorites from grade schoolers at Sni-A-Bar Elementary School in Grain Valley, Mo. The creative mind of a child is something special—especially when it comes to writing a letter to his or her favorite football player.

Dear Dunte Hall Do you like you are cool! are is it to be a Chiefs play the coch! can I have your sheff

82

Elizabet 3 Ba

Dear Danthall How long have you ben playing foot ball? You are avenys very popular foot ball player! I hope I can meet you! from Jessica Swindell Mrs. Halsall 2nd grade

82

you ROCK!

kc

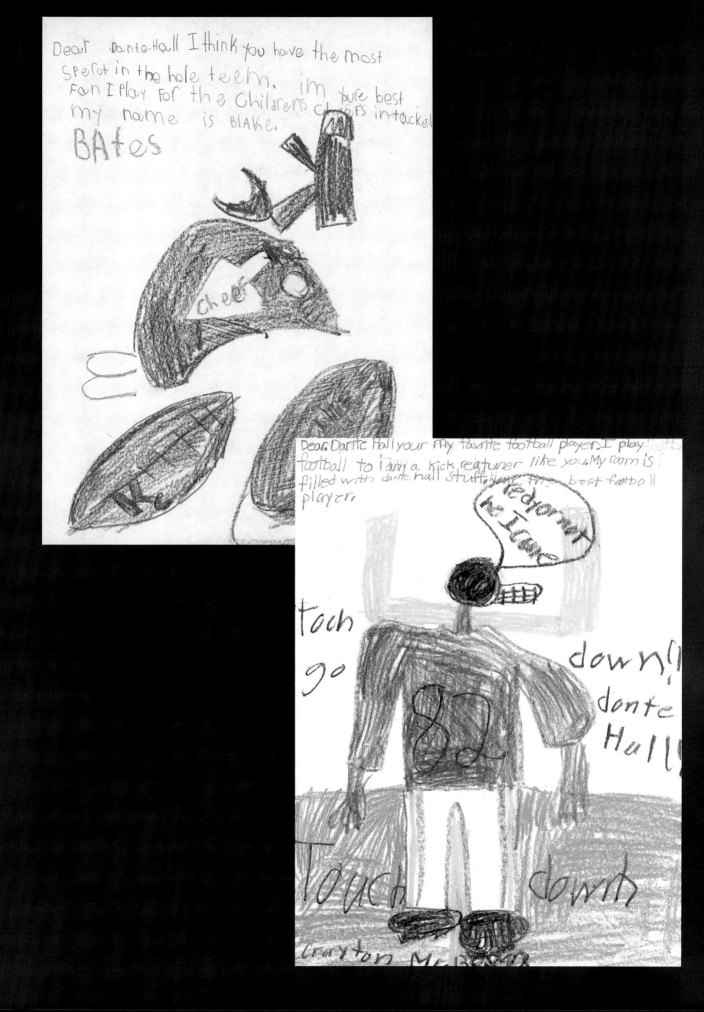

Dear Dante-Hall I think you have the most sperot in the hole teem. im yure best Fan I play For the Childrens cheefs in-tackel my name is BLAKe. BAtes

Dear. Dante Hall your my favrite football player. I play football to i am a Kick reaturner like you. My room is filled with dante hall stuff. your my best football player.

toch go

down!! dante Hall

Touch down

Crayton M

Dear, Dante Hall you are my favorite play
what is it like playing for the chiefs?
if you were to play on a nother team what would
it be? and if you were to play a nother
sport what would it be? from: Tayler Case

SCOr
Chiefs Other
39   0

Dante
Hall
T-Heme

Case
Mrs.
ss. Bates

Dear, Dante Hall
Hi. How are you? Do you
have a dog? My dad is
a big fann of the Chiefs
I like the Chiefs
too. Well got to go
big. from Michda
Fox
2nd grade
Mis. Bowm
class

3-19-04

Dear Dante Hall,
YOU are the Best player
in the chiefs history. I love
you guys. I go to school at
Sni-A-Bar. Did you?

Love, Stephen and Mrs.
Dixon

Dear Dante Hall,
You are my favorite chiefs player. I have two
brothers.
What is your favorite color. My favorite
is green and black. I'm in 2nd grade.

megan Dietz
2nd grade
Cackley

82

Dear Dante-hall,
I love the Chiefs! So do my parents.
You are my favorite football player! I go
to Sni-A-Bar Elementry, and I'm in 2nd grade.
How many players are there in your team?
How many times have the Chiefs won?
What sports do you like? What do you like
about football?

Rachel Snow Mrs. Brown's class 2nd grade

Dear Dantehall I like the chieffs.
The chieffs are very good.
You did a grate job.
Why do you like to play foot ball.
I am in secert grade.

You
rock!

Dear Dante Hall,   Mar. 16, 2004

I am your bigest Fan. I am your
Friend Hall

82

Zachar,

Teacher Mr. Huber

Dear Dante hall, my mom and dad are a
big fan. I think you're cool. You play really good.
My mom and dad yell when you make a touchdow
                          Mrs. Bates
From,
Cheyenne

AAA   AAA

2-St

3-15-04

Dear Dante Hall,
You are a really good player. How
I no that is becouse my Dad jumps
up and down and I watch football with
him. My name is Mikayla Alexander
and my teacher's name is Ms. Stidham.
Do you like playing football?

Your friend
Mikayla
Alexander

that's me!!

Dear DanteHalls

You are the best football
player in the world. You are
Rad. 82 is the coolest number.
I am 8 years old.

from Jordan-Nicole-Wilson   2-G

me

82 82 82 82 82
82   Dear Dante Hall,
82   I hav your shirt.   82
82   I am going to play takel 82
      next year, I wen tto   82
82   NFL to wocht you.
82   CodyHughesBowman

82

Dear Dante Hall,
How long have you ben plaing football?
My brother plays football.
I thank I can takuleyou.
I am your biget fan!
your fan Shelby

Kc

Shelby

CHAPTER

25

DEAR DIARY:
THE HALL OF FAME

I'm in the Hall of Fame! How about that. Well, it's not exactly the NFL Hall of Fame, it's the Scottish Claymores Hall of Fame. I was inducted April 18, prior to Scotland's 2004 NFL Europe home opener against the Amsterdam Admirals in Glasgow.

You really have to be a Dante Hall fan to know why I was inducted into the Claymores' Hall of Fame. I spent the 2001 season in Scotland and I remember it for two reasons—the fans and the beautiful countryside. (Claymore fans will remember it for his league-leading 24.4-yard kickoff return average and five touchdown receptions).

Without my NFL Europe experience, I wouldn't be in the NFL today. In this league, there isn't enough time in the day to get all of the necessary repetitions to get better. That is what NFL Europe is about. By going to Scotland, I was able to get game experience and get the reps in practice. I really felt like I was ready for the NFL when I went back to Kansas City. I was ready because of my experience over in Scotland. The old saying that hard work pays off is really true. I came to the Claymores, worked hard and did everything that was asked of me. During the season, I put out my best effort in the NFL Europe games and when I came back it paid off. If you work hard and give your best, nine times out of ten you will be rewarded.

I have a lot of fond memories of Glasgow and still have a lot of friends there. I'm not only looking forward to reporting for the NFL Network but also to catching up with all my friends and the fans in Scotland. There have been some friends who have encouraged me to visit them in Scotland, and now, I'm going to have the opportunity to do that.

The Claymores and NFL Europe is where it all started for me in 2001. Coming back to the Claymores is kind of like going back home to the place where I grew up. It is really where I grew up as a person and as a player in the NFL. It feels like I'm back home.

"YOU CAN'T EVER GET RELAXED WHEN YOU THINK HE'S GOING AWAY FROM YOU, BECAUSE IF HE FINDS A DEAD END OVER THERE HE'LL TURN AROUND AND BRING IT BACK THE OTHER WAY. AND THERE'S NO HESITATION ON HIS PART LOSING GROUND TO GET BACK OVER THERE."
—Marty Schottenheimer, San Diego Chargers coach

With fans signaling touchdown on the sidelines, Dante does his thing and scores another touchdown.

Scott E. Thomas photo